Journey to Data Quality

Journey to Data Quality

Yang W. Lee, Leo L. Pipino, James D. Funk, and
Richard Y. Wang

The MIT Press
Cambridge, Massachusetts
London, England

MIT Press books may be purchased at special quantity discounts for business or sales promotional use. For information, please e-mail ⟨special_sales@mitpress .mit.edu⟩ or write to Special Sales Department, The MIT Press, 55 Hayward Street, Cambridge, MA 02142.

This book was set in Sabon on 3B2 by Asco Typesetters, Hong Kong. Printed and bound in the United States of America.

Library of Congress Cataloging-in-Publication Data

Journey to data quality / Yang W. Lee ... [et al.].
    p.   cm.
Includes bibliographical references and index.
ISBN 10: 0-262-12287-1—ISBN 13: 978-0-262-12287-0 (alk. paper)
1. Business—Data processing—Management. 2. Database management—Quality control. I. Lee, Yang W.

HF5548.2.J68   2006
658.4′038—dc22   2006043331

10 9 8 7 6 5 4 3 2 1

Contents

Preface

This book represents the cumulative research and practice of the authors and many academicians and practitioners in industry and government. The book is a distillation of the ideas and concepts that have been presented in academic journals and at academic and practice conferences.

It is also a presentation of how these ideas have been adapted as principles, tools, techniques, and policies for practice in many organizations in their journey to data quality. Whenever feasible, we introduce specific real-world examples and industry cases to complement the discussions of the theoretical concepts and approaches.

The book is intended for business executives, data quality practitioners, researchers in data quality, and students. Practitioners will benefit from understanding the theoretical underpinnings of what they practice and thus become better equipped for future problem solving and practice. Researchers will benefit from reading how theories are actually put into practice, which in turn will help them focus on areas for further research. For students, the book in its entirety should provide a sound basis for future work and study in the field. Business executives should find the beginning chapters and the one on policy (chapter 11) of particular interest and help.

Acknowledgments

Many people have contributed to the publication of this book. We thank the anonymous reviewers who saw the intellectual and practical potential of the first draft and took great pains to help us realize a coherent book. We thank colleagues who reviewed this book and gave valuable feedback. Many researchers and practitioners collaborated in the previous research and consulting work that is a basis for this book. They are Stuart Madnick, Don Ballou, Harry Pazer, Giri Tayi, Diane Strong, Beverly Kahn, Elizabeth Pierce, Stanley Dobbs, and Shobha Chengular-Smith. Raïssa Katz-Haas and Bruce Davidson contributed the materials for many of the examples of data quality practice in this book.

Additionally, we thank the many industry practitioners who opened their practices and organizations as field laboratories for us.

Some of the work presented here is borrowed from previous publications by the authors. We appreciate the permission granted by *Communications of the ACM*, *Sloan Management Review*, *Prentice Hall*, *Journal of Management Information Systems*, *Journal of Database Management*, *Information and Management*, *International Journal of Healthcare Technology and Management*, and *IEEE Computer* to use this material.

Doug Sery at MIT Press patiently offered great vision and unreserved support to the idea of this book throughout the project.

This book could not have been completed without the productive work environment provided by the MIT Information Quality program, Cambridge Research Group, the MIT Total Data Quality Management (TDQM) program, and the following bright and devoted associates: Tony Nguyen, Karen Tran, Rith Peou, Andrey Sutanto, John Maglio, and Jeff Richardson. We also appreciate the support of Northeastern University's College of Business Administration. Thanks are also due to the College of Management at the University of Massachusetts Lowell for its support.

Finally, we thank our families for their love, support, and understanding during the prolonged time for working on this book. Albina Bertolotti, Marcella Croci, Karen Funk, Karalyn Smith, Marc Smith, Jacob Smith, Cameron Smith, Kirsten Ertl, Phil Ertl, Austin Ertl, Logan Ertl, Lorenzina Gustafson, Laura Gustafson, Juliana Gustafson, and Fori Wang brought so much joy and happiness to our lives. Not least, we would like to thank our parents, who instilled in us the love of learning.

Journey to Data Quality

1

Introduction

Jane Fine, Director of Information Systems at a global manufacturing company, sat at her desk contemplating her next move. Knowing the structure and content of the corporate databases, she anticipated that it would be difficult to answer reasonable questions from the marketing vice president regarding the total sales to a major client. She knew that the manner in which the company handled duplicate customer identifiers and duplicate product codes would make it difficult to answer the questions. It was clear that a problem existed.

A thousand miles away, Jim Brace, Senior Vice President of Medical Affairs at General Hospital, was confronting a different situation. He had just attended a meeting chaired by the hospital's CEO at which the attendees were informed that the state's regulatory commission had rejected the hospital's latest mandated report, questioning the validity of the data. The situation had to be rectified quickly. Rejection of the report would mean no state reimbursement of fees.

While reviewing personnel files, Dean Gary, Senior Information Specialist in a government human resources division, noticed a discrepancy between the raw data in some of the personnel files and the summary figures in the latest personnel report prepared by his division. Further probing revealed that there were inconsistencies in the data. The problem had not yet been noticed by the end users of the reports, nor had it been manifested in other ways, but it would not remain hidden forever.

In two of these cases the problems were discovered by upper managers in the information systems area. If the problems were allowed to persist, it would not be long before senior management discovered that a poor decision had been made based on poor-quality data. In General

Hospital's case, the CEO was made aware of a data quality problem by an agency external to the hospital.

In most companies, how to convince the CEO that a problem exists and that a formal data quality program should be instituted presents a challenge. For example, at the global manufacturing company, senior executives usually received the information they requested within a reasonable amount of time. As far as they were concerned, no problem existed. Unseen by the executives was the extra work that had to be undertaken in order to meet ad hoc requests and clean up inconsistencies in the data. Not evident was the time spent rectifying data quality problems, time that could have been used more productively at other tasks.

The managers in these three examples had to confront data quality problems in their organizations. We suspect that most organizations face similar challenges.

Can Information Be Shared?

Organizations often experience difficulties when they try to use information across business functions, system boundaries, or organization boundaries. They are frustrated when they believe they have the data to perform a business function and cannot do it. A firm may wish to perform a trend analysis or to build closer relationships with its customers or partnering organizations. All too often, the information technology department cannot provide the integrated information requested by the consumer or cannot deliver the needed information within the time frame required by the consumer. The opportunity to take advantage of the information the company has gathered and stored will have been lost. Even worse, what if their competitors were able to make strategic use of similar information faster?

These problems have confronted organizations for a long time. Data quality problems have manifested themselves in other ways, too. Examples of other situations include the following:

• Many global businesses have difficulty managing their data globally such that the data permits answering current and future global business questions as well as local business questions.

• External examinations such as regulatory commission reviews for cost reimbursement or any customer complaint bring internal data problems to the surface.
• Information systems projects reveal existing data problems, particularly those with cross-functional scope and multiple data sources.
• Organization members identify data problems during their ongoing work but use work-arounds to meet immediate needs and do not raise inquiries to create more permanent or sustainable solutions.

A New System Is Not the Answer

Organizations want to have high-quality data, but they don't have a road map to get to the state they desire. A course of action, too often adopted and later regretted, is to develop a new system to replace the old system. Firms often start with a clean slate in terms of systems but fail to address the data problems that were responsible for the difficulties in the first place. Typically the information systems department is immediately brought in to apply the newest technology, and a more popular or common hardware/software solution using the latest technology is developed. In this case we have a system-driven solution, that is, the development of the new system becomes the objective, not delivering high-quality data, not fixing the data quality problem. Indeed, it is quite probable that the new system will exacerbate the problem rather than solve it. Although on occasion a system solution is the proper one, usually the true drivers creating the problem are masked or further hidden.

Many organizations are led to believe that if they install the latest software package, such as an enterprise resource planning (ERP) system, or if they follow the trend and develop a data warehouse, they will achieve higher levels of data quality. Their hope is that with these systems in place they will be better able to share information across the enterprise. In the process of integrating data from different sources, however, it becomes clear that there are substantive inconsistencies in data definitions, data formats, and data values, and that time pressures will force the information technology department to continue the same bad data practices that existed before.

Many companies have been disappointed when their data warehousing efforts fail to deliver better business value. Many data warehousing efforts and ERP implementations have not delivered the business value initially promised and intended.

A global manufacturing company that we studied tried to aggregate information about sales on a global basis. Even though the company had the raw data, it took months to actually deliver a usable set of data that represented the needs of the business to work with selected customers on a global basis. Problems included multiple identifications for the same customer and the same designation identifying more than one customer. Additionally, the information stored in individual systems was not properly defined and documented from an enterprise perspective. Access to the physical databases was not always available. Definitions of concepts and terms were not standardized across the organization. For those occasions when standardization was not possible, the deviations from the standard were neither recorded nor shared.

At this stage, the company had expended a large part of the project budget. Would management be willing to augment the budget? Would management stop the project? If management did augment the budget, but the fundamental business and data quality issues were not addressed, would the situation change materially? Would the organization have committed to the creation of another business process and its associated costs that would not lead to increased business value? If management stopped the project, efforts to share information across the organization would not improve. Both courses of action would not lead to any increase in the overall data quality within the organization.

Most organizations have focused too narrowly on the systems side of the problem to the detriment of the data side of the problem. Addressing the data quality problems will lead to increased capability to share information across the organization. Without this focus most systems solutions will be prone to failure. What would a firm do if it recognized that it might have serious problems with data?

Some organizations use basic data-cleansing software to try to improve the quality of the data. In the case of the global manufacturing company, the initial cleanup resulted in a usable data warehouse. Over time, however, the quality of the data in the warehouse deteriorated significantly. Typically, in response to a data quality problem, an individual is appointed to address it, or an individual with an interest in it takes the initiative to address it. Regardless of how the problem is discovered or how the individual becomes the person responsible, the initial step is usually an ad hoc attempt to investigate what help is available.

Many organizations have used these ad hoc approaches and have encountered unsatisfactory results. Then any data quality initiatives are quickly brought to a halt. Unfortunately, restarting any data quality initiative in this situation will be very difficult. The bases for more systematic and comprehensive approaches are proposed in this book.

Starting the Data Quality Journey

Let's revisit the example scenarios to see what actions were taken. Jane Fine, at the global manufacturer, did some environmental scanning. Based on her knowledge of the database management and data quality fields, she began to investigate the state of the art in industry and academia, and to attend various seminars. She went to external sources in an attempt to acquire knowledge on how to approach the problem. The techniques and processes she deployed helped ameliorate the problem. Many challenges remained, however.

Jim Brace, supported by the General Hospital CEO, began by initiating an independent internal program in an attempt to solve the problem. This resulted in recommendations being made and implemented. Unfortunately, the data quality problems persisted, so Brace turned to the Total Data Quality Management literature and implemented the traditional improvement by measurement approach. This approach achieved some success: an external source of techniques and knowledge helped Brace take a proactive, more comprehensive approach and develop an ongoing, viable data quality program.

Dean Gary, in the human resources division, approached his problem using classic database integrity concepts and data-mining techniques. He applied a technical approach in trying to identify patterns of errors. This approach allowed him to eliminate the current problems. He was able to clean up the data that he received before using it in his analyses, allowing him to provide valid reports. What he could not do, however, was to identify and eliminate the root causes of the data inconsistencies. As a result, he was faced with repeating the data cleanup for every new data set received. He began looking for other approaches to improve data quality.

All three managers had embarked, knowingly or unknowingly, on the journey to data quality. Many alternative paths are available. If an appropriate path is taken, the journey will result in continuous improvement of data quality, although one can anticipate that new data quality problems will be discovered. This loop of problem finding, raising an inquiry, and problem solving will continue. Over the course of several iterations, the impact of poor data quality on the organization will decline dramatically. The iterations will continue, however. Solutions to problems will generate new problems, which will spur new inquiries, which will lead to defining new problems.

Stories of Successful Beginnings

Many organizations have embarked on their data quality journeys only to terminate them prematurely, thus never realizing the benefits of a sustained data quality effort. These quick terminations cause the organization to be plagued by persistent data quality problems. Too often these early terminations occur because of a lack of understanding of what can be expected on the journey, and they consequently lead to early discouragement and lack of perseverance. The organization should recognize that the current state of its data was not reached overnight. It should not expect that multiple problems developed over a long period of time will be solved quickly or as a single-point solution.

Returning to the example cases, we can trace how the managers each started at a different point, followed different paths toward the same end goal of long-term, sustainable data quality improvement, and adapted their approaches to fit their specific organization contexts.

Based on the results of her environmental scanning, Jane Fine, at the global manufacturing company, introduced a data quality awareness program. In addition, she initiated measurement of subjective assessment of the organization's data quality. She further measured the degree of data integrity in her inventory database. The results of the analysis led her to focus on the problem of data inconsistency. Having achieved some success, she was now able to answer questions such as what were the total sales of a specific product to major clients on a global basis. This success was recognized by senior managers and led to their directing her to institute a companywide data quality program. Fine again was contemplating her next move.

Dean Gary, at the government human resources division, was able to clean up the incoming data sets for purposes of preparing his reports. Repeatedly having to do this, however, led him to examine solutions that would eliminate the root causes of the data errors. These root causes involved external data source systems not under his direct control. His challenge now was to select a feasible approach.

Of the three, Jim Brace of General Hospital journeyed the furthest. Since he put the traditional Total Data Quality Management approaches in place, Brace had been able to present to management the concept of managing data as product, analogous to the process of manufacturing a physical product. Senior management endorsed this view and mandated that a data quality management working group be established. Further, senior management established data quality as an incentive-based corporate objective. In response, Brace proposed a data quality policy that was unanimously approved by the board of directors. With a data quality working group and an articulated data quality policy in place, he moved to develop a data production map that would help deal with the data quality problems detected by the state's regulatory commission.

As these examples illustrate, each manager faced different challenges and mounted responses to these challenges. To sustain long-term improvement in data quality and to institutionalize a sound data quality practice, however, it takes more than just individual managers who are committed to transforming their organization's data quality practice. Corporate executives must be on board to chart the course. It is heartening that the uppermost executive levels are increasingly becoming involved in data quality initiatives. The importance of commitment to data quality by the CEO cannot be overstated.

The CEO Leads the Journey

The CEO must provide the vision for the journey toward data quality. It is easy to relegate data quality initiatives to a low priority among projects and initiatives competing for scarce resources. Often the CEO never realizes the true magnitude of the problems caused by poor data quality. Ironically, behind the CEO is often an army of staff working hard to resolve data quality problems—a very expensive proposition at the corporate suite. There are many reasons for a CEO's becoming aware of the need to support data quality initiatives. It could be a crisis caused by using data of poor quality. For example, in the case of Jim Brace, when the state's regulatory commission rejected the hospital's latest mandated report and questioned the validity of the data, the letter was addressed to the CEO. Taking pride in the reputation of their high-quality service and the prestige of the hospital, the CEO and his senior management team personally approved a data quality initiative with strategic goals and objectives. The CEO may encounter the problem directly when he or she cannot obtain the information requested, when conflicting data are presented, or when erroneous data are used for a decision.

Barring a crisis or catastrophic event, it will take repeated communications of examples and solid arguments based on rigorous analysis and reasoning to convince the CEO to undertake data quality initiatives. Among the supporting analyses will have to be a convincing value proposition or cost/benefit analysis. Having the CEO's full support, however, will contribute mightily to a successful journey.

The Challenges of the Journey

The challenges of the journey will be many and difficult. We have identified one of the first and perhaps most formidable challenges: obtaining CEO buy-in and support for data quality initiatives. We also mentioned the need to develop a strong economic argument, a cost/benefit analysis, to support undertaking data quality initiatives. Promoting data quality awareness throughout the organization is a third challenge.

Having upper management support is the first step in developing data quality awareness in the firm. Developing this awareness requires developing new perspectives that extend and depart from the conventional views of data quality.

This requires a clear understanding of what the organization means by data quality and why it is important. In data quality workshops the issue of what is the difference between data and information, and between information and knowledge, is often raised. These three concepts are different. One could view them as forming a hierarchy whereby knowledge subsumes information, and information subsumes data. But drawing an arbitrary distinction between data and information will distract from the primary task and further mask understanding of a complex information production system.

Managers typically use the traditional distinction between data and information: data comprises raw facts or materials, and information is data that have been processed. One person's data, however, may be another's information. In one information system, for example, the input is raw data and the output is information, but if the output is then fed into another information system, then this output information would also be input data. Whether input data is the product (output) of a previous process is not necessarily known at all times. Because such ambiguities sooner or later arise, and because making the distinction is not material to the policies and techniques we discuss here, we use the terms *data* and *information* interchangeably throughout this book.

Data Quality: Why Is It Important?

In any organization it is critical that the importance of data quality be properly explained. From the CEO to the lower managerial levels, a sensible and understandable rationale must be given in order to obtain buy-in and motivate active participation in the data quality effort. Among the commonly used rationales are

- Data of high quality is a valuable asset.
- Data of high quality can increase customer satisfaction.
- Data of high quality can improve revenues and profits.
- Data of high quality can be a strategic competitive advantage.

Beyond these broad rationales, more specific ones can be offered.

To repeat an old aphorism, "An ounce of prevention is worth a pound of cure." In the context of customer relationship management, the cost of preventing an existing customer from defecting is only a fraction of that required to obtain a new customer. Organizations must not only develop tools and techniques to rectify data deficiencies but also institutionalize processes that would identify and prevent root causes of poor data quality. Awareness will require that a firm quantitatively measure both subjective and objective variables of data quality. A realistic, usable data quality policy will be required as part of the data quality journey.

Intuitive characterizations of the state of data quality will not do. A U.S. Supreme Court justice once said about what constitutes pornography, "I know it when I see it." Indeed, data quality is hard to define, measure, analyze, and improve, but just "knowing" its state when seeing it is no longer enough. Can the CEO certify that the quality of the organization's data conforms to specifications and meets or exceeds data consumers' expectations? Increasingly in today's business and government reporting environment, CEOs must meet this challenge. For instance, we see existing legislation, the Sarbanes-Oxley Act of 2002, that requires certification of financial reports and figures by the CEO.

Beyond legislative requirements, a compelling case can be made for committing the organization to the attainment of high-quality data: first-mover advantage, among others. It is precisely because it is difficult to meet the challenge for high-quality data and to sustain high-quality data that CEOs who meet the challenge will be richly rewarded with more accurate, believable, and timely data for their organization's activities. It would enable the firm to increase market share and maintain market leadership, act promptly on new business opportunities, and undertake preemptive strikes on potential threats to the organization's survival. These, in turn, translate into increased gross revenues, net profits, and corporate image. Because it is hard to meet the challenge, the entry barrier is high, and therefore the competitive advantage gained could be better sustained.

In sum, CEOs must act now to provide a vision for the journey to data quality. The stakes are high, and the journey will not be easy. Winners will pride themselves that they have led the journey to data quality and have succeeded in transforming their organizations to a new culture in which high-quality data is as fundamental as utilities such as electricity and drinkable tap water. The winners will also maintain their advantages as first-movers for opportunities to innovate, enabling them to lead and dominate the market.

Overview of the Book

We introduced the journey to data quality using three representative cases. We argued that involvement at the highest levels and awareness of data quality are necessary first steps in the journey to data quality. In the remainder of the book we provide principles, tools, techniques, and case examples that should help the organization in its journey.

In chapter 2 we discuss cost/benefit analysis and its use in making the economic case for data quality. Currently in industry this is often referred to as making the value proposition. Chapter 3 gives an overview of three approaches to assessing an organization's data quality. It then focuses on the subjective evaluation of an organization's data quality by three major stakeholders: data collectors, data custodians, and data consumers—the three Cs. A survey tool to perform the subjective evaluation is provided in this chapter. Chapter 4 discusses metrics that can be used to perform objective measurements of different data quality dimensions. Further, it introduces techniques and a software tool that can be used to assess the quality of data in a database.

Chapter 5 presents an overview of how the database can be audited by introducing relevant sampling techniques and additional strategies to estimate values for the metrics suggested in the previous chapter. Since data quality is multidimensional and the perspectives of the three Cs will not only evolve over time but will change relative to each other over time, organizations must define their data quality in context. A treatment of this is presented in chapter 6, where we also present a set of root conditions and how these can evolve over different paths. We also discuss interventions that can be initiated to avoid undesirable patterns that lead to data quality problems.

Chapter 7 presents a real-world case dealing with uncovering data quality problems in a health care organization. Chapter 8 follows with a discussion of a key perspective fundamental to successful data quality management: treating information as product, not by-product. We present four principles for managing information as product, principles that are derived from business cases that we have studied over the decade.

Chapter 9 presents the basic concepts of information product maps (IP-Maps) and elaborates on the creation and use of these maps. Chapter 10 presents a real-world case in which many of the principles and practices, particularly IP-Maps, were applied. Chapter 11 addresses data quality policy and discusses prescriptions that an organization should follow. An assessment instrument is provided to evaluate the data quality practice and product of an organization.

One might conclude that the journey ends with chapter 11. This is not so, as our concluding chapter 12 pronounces. The journey to data quality is never ending. As old problems are solved, new problems and new environments arise, and the journey continues. Chapter 12 briefly surveys new challenges, issues, and techniques, some still in the development stage, that will emerge in data quality research and practice.

One hopes that experience and knowledge will increase with each iteration of the journey, making each iteration less intimidating. The continuing journey will never be easy, but it will be rewarding.

2

Cost/Benefit Analysis

No business undertaking will endure without an economic justification. A thorough cost/benefit analysis is critical to any data quality program. Early on, perhaps before but certainly immediately after, any kickoff meetings and motivational exhortations, the executive team will require an economic justification—the value proposition underlying data quality and a data quality program. It is this economic rationale for the added value brought by good data quality or at the very least identification of opportunities and competitive advantages lost by poor data quality, that will support the other initiatives necessary to achieve awareness and to implement a viable data quality program. Indeed, the means to perform the necessary measurements described in chapters 3, 4, and 5 will not be provided without some degree of economic justification.

The Challenge

Executives are often unaware of data quality problems, or they tend to believe that the information technology department can handle the problems without the allocation of critical time and resources from the top level. The problems may be masked by one or more layers of subordinates, whose time and effort are spent searching for data whose accessibility is low or correcting errors and inconsistencies across functions (lack of shareability). The CEO obtains the data requested and remains unaware of the cost of producing it. Consequently, executives are reluctant to commit scarce resources to an apparent nonproblem unless there is a defensible cost/benefit justification to show the costs of neglecting the data quality problem and the economic benefits of initiating the data quality project. Senior executives may be further reluctant if the organization is performing adequately, particularly if calling attention to the problem would affect the corporate image. Senior management may not realize that poor data quality has a direct impact on the organization's performance.

The negative impact of poor data quality on companies has been documented in industry (Redman 1996; English 1999). Data quality problems result in lower customer satisfaction and increased costs. It has been estimated that data quality problems can cost companies as much as 8–12 percent of revenue in industry (Redman 1996). Often the magnitude of these problems may be unclear, unquantified, or unrecognized by managers who have become accustomed to accepting the cost associated with data quality problems as the "normal cost of doing business" (English 1999). Because organizations must be sensitive to the bottom line, usable and defensible cost/benefit analyses must be performed. A good analysis of the business impact of data quality can highlight critical areas for change and improvement.

The economic analysis can serve as the basis for any data quality effort; it can raise awareness of data quality and the costs of poor data quality. Such an analysis is not a trivial undertaking, particularly if it is the first time it has been undertaken. The first time one may not have any benchmark case to use as a reference or guide. If feasible, one might go outside the firm to find such a best-practice analysis. However it is done, such an analysis must be performed. Poor data quality will cause a firm to lose competitive advantage, if not immediately, certainly over the long term. The challenge is to relate the lack of data quality awareness and data quality effort as directly as possible to the loss of competitive advantage.

Costs incurred are typically easier to quantify than benefits. Typically, many benefits are intangible. Further, benefits accruing from the implementation of new technology, improved procedures, and improved data are diffused throughout the organization's operations and are not easily related directly to the data quality initiative. Although intangible costs do arise, these are far fewer than intangible benefits. As indicated, an added challenge arises when the analysis is performed for the first time in that no benchmarks exist within the firm to help in performing and assessing the analysis.

Benefits accrued by cost avoidance or cost savings can be quantified when identified. The exercise of identifying these savings can itself be enlightening with respect to how the organization is operating, the effects of data quality on operations, and the overall awareness of the importance of data quality to the organization.

As strong as the cost avoidance benefits may be, and as much as they may outweigh the costs incurred, this may not sway senior management. At this level, management's focus may be on the cost of undertaking a data quality initiative, and management may place less weight on the eventual cost savings. We discuss just such a situation later in this chapter.

To perform the analysis of quantifiable costs versus quantifiable benefits a number of classical techniques can be employed. Such financial/accounting approaches as net present value analysis, payback, and internal rate of return are available. In essence, when using these techniques, one treats the cost/benefit analysis as a traditional capital budgeting problem. It is important to note, however, that these techniques rest on the premise that one has hard, solid numbers and a good estimate of the cost of capital. Even with hard numbers for costs and benefits, if the value of cost of capital assumed proves to be erroneous, the analysis can lead to suspect recommendations. On the positive side, it should be noted that these methods are widely accepted and used.

Other, more complex and analytically sophisticated, techniques can also be employed. These will require a substantive investment in time to develop and to obtain the necessary parameter values. If time is a constraint, they may be infeasible to use. In addition, these techniques may require continual adjustment in the face of a rapidly changing economic and competitive environment. We introduce two such techniques later in this chapter. The first is based on the options pricing model, the real options approach. The second is associated with the concept of information product and makes use of a data flow model.

The Cost/Benefit Trade-off

In this section we review some standard approaches to cost/benefit analysis and give some examples of the approaches taken by different organizations.

A straightforward approach to assess the economic trade-offs of undertaking a data quality program, one used often to evaluate information systems projects, is to quantify the benefits and costs and to apply the basic value relationship:

Value = Benefits − Costs.

The challenge reduces to how well one can quantify costs and benefits, what assumptions are made in weighing the two, and how one incorporates intangible benefits into the analysis.

Typically, one would capture the direct costs, such as labor expenses, hardware, and software needed to undertake and sustain a data quality effort. Indirect or overhead costs must also be included. One should always be aware of hidden costs. On the benefits side, one would attempt to quantify benefits as well as to capture the intangible benefits. Most likely, the tangible quantifiable benefits will consist of cost savings, that is, the dollars saved by avoiding identifiable data quality problems. In addition, it may be possible to quantify other benefits that increase the competitiveness of the firm and as a consequence contribute to the bottom line. This latter condition, however, is most difficult to do, and the opportunity to do so will not be frequent.

In what follows we summarize how a number of organizations and data quality practitioners approach the value proposition task. In particular, we focus on the costs and benefits of what these organizations suggest should be measured. It is hoped that this summary will be informative and help the reader to develop his own relevant list.

With the costs and benefits captured, the standard capital budgeting methods, such as net present value discounting, internal rate of return, or payback can be used. Many organizations specify exactly which method should be employed. For example, the U.S. Department of Defense (DoD) specifies net present value discounting in evaluating information systems projects and further specifies the discount rate to be used.

Each organization has a preferred technique, which may be simple or quite complex. For example, a data quality company used a somewhat qualitative approach in the absence of hard numbers. The company indicated that "if you have the solid number, such as financial savings or increase in revenue to tie to improved information, then by all means use it, but if you don't, do not despair, you can get along without it." There-fore, the justifications proposed are mostly qualitative, such as consistent answers to questions, eliminating duplication of efforts, or preserving knowledge assets. For most companies, the intangible benefits, clearly stated, provided sufficient justification. The reader should recognize, however, that to some senior executives, a list of intangible benefits, however compelling, will not be sufficient without some hard numbers.

The DoD has a comprehensive set of guidelines on data quality man-agement (Cykana, Paul, and Stern 1996). Four types of causes for data quality problems are identified: (1) process problems refer to problems in data entry, assignment, execution, and data exchange, (2) system prob-lems come from undocumented or unintended system modifications, or incomplete user training and manuals, (3) policy and procedure prob-lems refer to conflict or inappropriate guidance, and (4) database design problems occur as result of incomplete data constraints.

The DoD guidelines suggest that costs arising from data quality prob-lems should be evaluated from two perspectives: the costs of correcting them and the costs of not correcting them. Costs attributable to poor data quality include direct costs from operational failures, which are esti-mated through labor hours and machine hours, and indirect costs result-ing from damage to the customer relationship or the brand. The indirect costs are intangible. Eliminating them would be considered intangible benefits. That these costs exist is known. To quantify them, however, is very difficult.

English (1999) has suggested three categories of costs: (1) costs of non-quality information, (2) costs of assessment or inspection, and (3) costs associated with process improvement and defect prevention. Included in the costs of nonquality of information would be process failure costs, li-ability and exposure costs, information scrap and rework costs, and lost and missed opportunity costs. A number of English's costs can be consid-ered cost avoidance, or benefits. For example, eliminating information scrap and rework costs would be considered a cost savings and, as such, a benefit in the value equation. Among those costs, assessment or inspec-tion costs could potentially create value by reducing errors, while process improvement costs will provide the highest benefits. The costs of low-quality information are further analyzed from the two perspectives of business process and customer relationship.

A conceptual framework to classify costs related to low data quality has been suggested by Eppler and Helfert (2004). They develop a taxonomy of data quality costs, classifying them into two main categories: (1) costs caused by low data quality, and (2) costs of improving or assuring data quality. Category 1 can be further subdivided into direct and indirect costs, each of which can be further subdivided. Direct costs consist of verification costs, reentry costs, and compensation costs. Indirect costs consist of costs based on lower reputation, costs based on wrong decisions or actions, and sunk investment costs. Category 2 can be subdivided into prevention costs, detection costs, and repair costs. Again, each of these can be further subdivided. Prevention costs consist of training costs, monitoring costs, and standard development and deployment costs. Detection costs consist of analysis costs and reporting costs. Repair costs consist of repair planning costs and repair implementation costs.

A Case Example

We use the case of a real-world, not-for-profit organization to illustrate a straightforward, traditional approach to cost/benefit analysis and the challenges faced in advancing a data quality program even when the quantitative analysis lends strong support to undertaking the program.

NFP (a pseudonym) is a large nonprofit organization consisting of multiple units operating around the globe. Each unit is tasked with a specific mission but at the same time they are required to participate in joint projects. Since NFP operates on a worldwide basis, it also has set up centralized services that support the different units and their projects. One such centralized advisory unit is the central information systems group. One of the data quality challenges that NFP faces is maintaining consistent reference tables. For example, a location reference table would have a short unique code for each country. There are a number of different standards that could be used. At NFP each unit is responsible for maintaining its own reference tables. Inconsistency in reference table values or use of different standards in maintaining a particular type of reference table can lead to lack of coordination between units. For example, if this involves shipment of goods from one unit to another, use of inconsistent reference tables could incur costs of correcting for the shipping of material to the wrong location.

To address the problem, NFP recently experimented with a new approach and system to validate and maintain reference tables by doing a pilot study with one of its units. At about the same time, NFP set up a central corporate information systems unit. As part of its data quality effort, NFP was considering making the central information unit the validator of all reference table sources and the distributor of updated information. Each unit would still be required to update its tables using the pilot system, but as was not the case before, all would be using the same information for sources and updates.

NFP performed a cost/benefit analysis as part of an overall system feasibility analysis in order to determine whether rolling out the new system throughout the organization was justified. The cost/benefit analysis entailed capturing all the costs that would be incurred. The tangible benefits that would accrue were actually cost savings and cost avoidance. These benefits or cost reductions derived from such factors as reduction of duplicate efforts, elimination of multiple subscription fees for the same subscription, and reduction in the cost of validating and verifying the different systems. NFP analyzed the costs and benefits over a five-year period using the net present value discounting method to make the numbers for each year comparable. The spreadsheet in figure 2.1 illustrates the analysis. For proprietary reasons, the actual numbers have been changed, but the numbers do reflect the actual ratio of costs to benefits.

Although the absolute values of costs were high, the tangible benefits far outweighed the costs. In addition, NFP was able to clearly identify a number of intangible benefits, which were accepted as valid. Taken all together, a good "story" had been developed to be presented to senior management.

One would expect that the effort would have been immediately embraced. This was not to be the case. Upper management was focused on the cost side of the equation. As a consequence, even though the benefits, both tangible and intangible, clearly outweighed the costs and were accepted at face value, management felt the cost was too high. In short, the decision criterion was the magnitude of the costs regardless of

COSTS

	Hardware	Software	Software Development	Database Design & Setup	System Analysis & Manage Tables	Personnel & Facilities	Subscriptions	TOTAL per Year
Set Up	$ 29,000	$ 190,000	$ -	$ 2,000	$ -	$ 800	-	$ 221,800
FY04-05	$ 17,000	$ 6,000	$ 20,000	$ -	$ 405,000	$ 8,000	$ 11,000.00	$ 467,000
FY05-06	$ 27,000	$ 7,000	$ 4,000	$ -	$ 820,000	$ 17,000	$ 12,000.00	$ 887,000
FY06-07	$ 78,000	$ 95,000	$ 4,000	$ -	$ 1,199,000	$ 26,000	$ 13,000.00	$ 1,415,000
FY07-08	$ 22,000	$ 9,000	$ 4,000	$ -	$ 1,522,000	$ 33,000	$ 13,000.00	$ 1,603,000
FY08-09	$ 20,000	$ 9,800	$ 4,000	$ -	$ 1,804,000	$ 39,000	$ 12,000.00	$ 1,888,800

First 5 Yrs Total $ 6,482,600

BENEFITS

	First Time		Recurring		
	System Analysis	New Manage Tables	System Analysis	Manage Tables	TOTAL
Starting 04	Already analyzed 300 tables & 110 systems				
FY04-05	$ 220,000	$ 469,000	$ -	$ 306,000	$ 995,000
FY05-06	$ 220,000	$ 433,000	$ -	$ 1,635,000	$ 2,288,000
FY06-07	$ 220,000	$ 325,000	$ -	$ 3,578,000	$ 4,123,000
FY07-08	$ 220,000	$ 244,000	$ -	$ 4,731,000	$ 5,195,000
FY08-09	$ 220,000	$ 183,000	$ -	$ 5,596,000	$ 5,999,000

First 5 Yrs Total $ 18,600,000

Total Costs Over 5 Years	$ 6,482,600
Discount Rate	$ 4.50%
Overall Present Value of Costs	$ 5,580,785

Total Net Benefits Over 5 Years	$ 18,600,000
Discount Rate	$ 4.50%
Overall Present Value of Benefits	$ 15,830,544

Overall ROI for First 5 Years	184%

Figure 2.1
NFP Cost/Benefit Analysis

benefits. To justify the effort, then, other systemic changes would have to be made in order to make the costs more palatable to management. Another obstacle was NFP's makeup. Each unit was more than willing to transition to a new system as long as it would not have to contribute dollars to the effort. As long as the central information systems would bear the cost of the data quality program, there would not be a problem, assuming discipline could be enforced. The individuals units, however, were less than enthusiastic about the effort when they were faced with allocating a portion of their budgets to the effort.

Ideally, the logic of the economic argument should have carried the day. Unfortunately, the NFP case highlights a number of issues that the advocate of a data quality program will face. Most likely, many readers can readily identify with these issues, having had to confront them. The bias of many executives toward cost, or more precisely, toward reducing cost, leads to their putting less weight on future gains that will not be immediately realized. In short, they take a short-term view. Further, obtaining the buy-in of different operating units, each of which will incur a charge against its budget, may be very difficult. The units may see the need, but when confronted with having to fund some of the work, many functional units can always find "better" ways to spend the money. Last, the economic analysis may lead to systemic changes, that is, reengineering of processes, simply because the imperative of reducing the magnitude of the costs, even when greatly outweighed by the benefits, require it in order to proceed with the program.

Further Cost/Benefit Analysis Techniques

The cost/benefit analyses discussed in the previous sections reflect the standard approaches making use of the classical systems development life cycle, often outlined in information systems textbooks. Other techniques that are analytically more intensive and specialized may also be used. Two that we briefly discuss in this section are the real options approach and the data quality flow model (DQFM). The application of these models to data quality remains in the developmental stage. Nevertheless, the basic ideas and constructs used in these models may be of use to the analyst when performing economic analyses.

Real Options

Real options are an extension of financial pricing theory to real assets. The approach evolved from developments in financial theory, in particular, the well-known Black-Scholes (1973) model. It can be applied to diverse business problems. More recently, it has been suggested as a preferred method to evaluate information systems projects. Research in this area is continuing.

We suggest that it can be used to evaluate a proposed data quality program analogous to evaluating the investments in an organization's infrastructure or evaluating the development of new drugs or evaluating oil exploration projects. Recent, research into prioritizing information technology projects using the technique has been reported (Bardhan, Bagchi, and Sougstad 2004). If data quality initiatives in the corporation are classified as information technology projects, then real options can be used to evaluate and prioritize data quality projects as part of an overall information systems portfolio.

Amram and Kulatilaka (1998) present a four-step solution process that constitutes the real options approach:

1. *Frame the application.* This consists of identifying such things as the key decisions, the options available, and the areas of uncertainty.
2. *Implement the option evaluation model.* This consists of establishing the inputs to the model and choosing a specific model.
3. *Review the results.* This involves reviewing the results, comparing them against benchmarks, then using this information in the next step.
4. *Redesign.* Based on the results, decide if redesign is necessary and, if so, examine alternatives and possibly expand the alternatives.

Amram and Kulatilaka emphasize that step 2 is crucial. This requires the implementation of an option evaluation model. These same authors point out that there are three general solutions to calculating the value of options: (1) a closed-form solution that involves the solution of a partial differential equation, (2) a dynamic programming solution, and (3) use of simulation models. These are general solution methods that have been used for engineering and business problems. Each of these are analytically and computationally intensive. The details of each method are beyond the scope of this book.

The application of these ideas to a portfolio of information technology projects, specifically, to the problem of prioritizing a set of projects, has been reported by Cochran (1997). The approach makes use of a nested options model that takes into account the interdependencies among the projects when calculating option values. Application of the concepts of real options to the evaluation of one specific data quality project in stand-alone mode was reported at the ninth International Conference on Information Quality (Bobrowski and Vazquez-Soler 2004).

These specific endeavors as well as the more general application of real option techniques to data quality project evaluation require a high degree of analytical and computational sophistication. The analyst must decide whether the investment in time, effort, and model building justifies using the technique or whether the standard discounted present values are sufficient. A similar question must be answered with respect to using the DQFM model.

Data Quality Flow Model

In chapters 8 and 9 we present in detail the concept of information as product and the formalisms of information product maps. A model that is related to information product maps and predates them was introduced by Wang, Ziad, and Lee (2001). It is the Data Quality Flow Model (DQFM). We briefly introduce it here because the model and its formalisms were developed to aid in the computation of revenues attributable to data quality. As will be seen in chapter 9, the formalisms of IP-Maps subsume this model. Nevertheless, the DQFM is an alternative approach to those previously introduced in this chapter. It may aid the analyst in developing her own variation. The material in this section is based on Wang, Reddy, and Kon (1995).

The DQFM is designed to analyze the business impact of data quality. The representation of data flows and processes are similar to those of the traditional data flow diagram model. The DQFM adopts a queuing network approach, based on the work of Jackson (1963), to compute revenues (or loss of revenues) of a complex network of flows and processing units or servers. The model allows one to compute the incremental cost of data quality problems and the effects of various configurations to correct these problems. It may be used to evaluate the addition of various quality improvement schemes. It introduces a method for evaluating the business impact of data quality in dollar terms. Note that the final trade-off between costs and benefits, however, is performed using the basic technique of net present value discounting.

The DQFM makes use of three basic constructs: data quality flows, processing units, and control units. A data quality flow (DQF) describes a flow of records or transactions through the system. Each flow is uniquely identified by its type of potential data quality problem. A basic assumption is that DQFs are mutually exclusive. Multiple error occurrences will normally be categorized into one of several possible flow categories. In practice, this is obviously not a valid assumption, although records with one error type may be corrected for that defect and then recounted in a second category on their second trip through the system. For simplicity, the multiple error occurrence is ignored. For measurement and impact analysis, this may not be a poor approximation when dealing with small error rates.

Figure 2.2 illustrates a very simple DQFM example. A DQF may be those records containing invalid customer addresses (call it the Invalid-Address flow), as shown in the figure. It does not necessarily represent a distinct physical flow or path of records. At some stage in the information system, however, this DQF can be expected to undergo a different flow from that of correct records. Usually, this rerouting is due to a detected quality problem. If the error is immediately corrected at low cost, then this type of error in the DQF may not even be included. In any case, there will be at least one DQF, the Correct DQF, in every information system.

A processing unit (PU) represents some action by a person or a computer that transforms, transmits, or reroutes DQFs. A PU is uniquely identified and, in the notation we use, the physical agent involved in the PU is listed. Frequently there is a cost associated with a PU. An example of a PU might be Fill-Form, which involves the completion of a form. By convention, the actors involved in the PU are identified. For instance, the actors System and User perform Fill-Form.

A control unit (CU) is a special type of PU representing some action by a person or a computer that inspects, verifies, and corrects DQFs. A CU may reroute or eliminate a DQF altogether by mapping it back to the Correct DQF. Note that the Correct DQF cannot normally be eliminated. A CU is uniquely identified. An example of a CU might be Check-Form, which involves the verification and possible reentry of a form. In

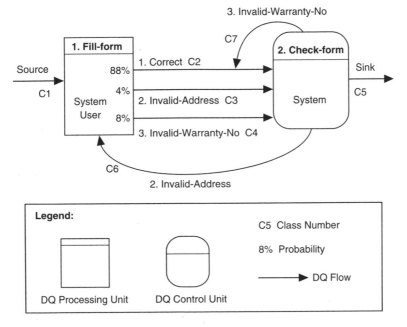

Figure 2.2
Data Quality Flow Model (DQFM) Example
Source: C. Firth, *Management of the Information Product*, master's thesis, Massachusetts Institute of Technology, 1993.

our example, this check is performed by the system and requires a repeat of Fill-Form. Thus, in our example, the flow Invalid-Address loops back to the Fill-Form PU. This configuration implies errors can be reintroduced even though the user is aware of the original problem.

These flows can be represented in equation form with appropriate probabilities to compute expected costs and revenues. We refer the reader to Wang, Reddy, and Kon (1995) for the detailed formulations. As with the real options approach, this method will be analytically intensive. The organization must decide on the appropriateness of the approach for the cost/benefit trade-off at hand.

Concluding Remarks

Performing cost/benefit analyses as part of the decision to undertake or not undertake projects has long been a standard prescription for all types of projects. These analyses are not easy to perform and are almost always performed in an environment of uncertainty. This is particularly true for information systems projects, of which the initiation of data quality projects and programs are a part.

In this chapter we reviewed some standard techniques for comparing benefits and costs. As part of this review, we listed a number of different costs and benefits that can be assessed when performing cost/benefit analyses. In addition, we briefly introduced and referenced two relatively sophisticated analytical models that can be used to evaluate the business impact of data quality. If undertaken, these analyses will be labor-intensive and require analytical sophistication.

With cost/benefit analysis in hand, the data quality analyst will be better able to articulate the value proposition of instituting a data quality program and the effects of such a program on the firm's competitive position.

3

Assessing Data Quality, Part I

How good is your organization's data? How does your organization analyze and improve the quality of its data? Assessment of data quality affects much beyond improving the quality of data. It involves data, the related transaction and reporting systems, and those business processes that are involved in collecting, storing, and using organizational data. Assessing organizational data, therefore, is critical for improving organizational decision making, strategy setting, and organizational performance. Any new systems reengineering or enterprise systems projects, benefit from assessment of organizational data quality.

In the context of data quality initiatives, data quality assessment provides a means of comparison by developing a baseline and periodically assessing the status across databases, stakeholders, and organizations. It can also serve as a basis from which to choose the most critical areas for improvement. Last, it provides the foundation on which a comprehensive data quality program can be initiated within the organization.

Chapters 3 and 4 introduce various techniques to assess data quality. We highlight how these assessment techniques are applied to form different data quality assessment approaches in practice. The three major techniques are

- Use of a data quality survey
- Use of quantifiable data quality metrics
- Embedding data integrity analysis in the Total Data Quality Management (TDQM) cycle

This chapter focuses on details of applying the data quality survey and analyzing and interpreting the results. Chapter 4 focuses on data quality metrics and the use of data integrity analysis within the TDQM cycle.

The TDQM cycle consists of define, measure, analyze, and improve (Total Data Quality Management Research Program, 1999).

Assessment Techniques and Associated Approaches

The data quality survey elicits evaluations of multiple data quality dimensions from multiple stakeholders in the organization. The resulting assessment reflects the perceptions of each of the respondents. The quantifiable data quality metrics are objective measurement formulas to assess data quality. The organization develops a collectively agreed-on metric for each data quality dimension. These metrics are then repeatedly applied. Data integrity analysis focuses on direct assessment of adherence to integrity constraints in the database. These assessments are performed within the context of the TDQM cycle. Appropriate application of database principles in practice includes conformance to all data integrity rules, including user-defined data integrity. This technique is less intrusive and initially may not require direct involvement of data consumers.

Different strategies employing combinations of these techniques can be adopted to assess the organization's data quality. We introduce three such approaches along with application of the strategies in practice.

The first is a comparative approach, first introduced by Pipino, Lee, and Wang (2002), which makes use of the data quality survey and quantifiable data quality metrics. This analysis compares the data collected from the surveys (perceptions of each class of stakeholder) and the results of the quantitative metrics. The resulting comparisons are used to diagnose and prioritize key areas for improvement. We often refer to it as the diagnostic approach because of its diagnostic nature and in order to distinguish it from an alternative comparative approach.

An alternative comparative approach uses aggregated results of data quality surveys to analyze and prioritize key areas of improvement. It includes gap analysis and benchmark analysis. Here the comparisons are not between two techniques. Making use of the survey technique, comparisons are made across stakeholders (collector, custodian, consumer) against an industry standard or another best-practice organization. This approach falls within the broader category of the AIMQ methodology (Lee et al., 2002).

A third approach, first introduced by Lee et al. (2004), embeds data integrity analysis into the process-oriented TDQM cycle. It maintains a chronological record of the results of data integrity analysis over time for data quality projects. This historical record allows the organization to adapt to a changing environment and maintain a continuing data quality improvement program.

All of these techniques can be adapted and tailored to an organization's individual needs and goals.

Assessment Approaches in Practice

Comparative Approach: Subjective and Objective Assessments

The diagnostic approach to data quality analysis consists of three steps: (1) perform data quality survey and measure data quality using data quality metrics, (2) compare the results of the two assessments, identify discrepancies, and determine root causes of discrepancies, and (3) determine and take necessary actions for improvement.

Ideally, information reflecting the degree to which a company has in place mechanisms to ensure the quality of information and the degree of knowledge among the different stakeholders regarding these mechanisms should be available as input to the comparative analysis. Although perhaps not mandatory, such input enhances the comparative analysis and aids in the evaluation of discrepancies and root causes. The method is depicted in figure 3.1.

To begin the analysis, the survey result and metrics measurement of a specific dimension are compared. To accomplish this phase, the organization must have a clear idea of what variables (data quality dimensions) are of importance. An assessment of the data quality along these dimensions must be obtained from each of the three stakeholder groups: data collectors, data custodians, and data consumers. The same dimensions used in the survey should also be measured as objectively as possible. This will entail developing quantitative metrics for the stipulated dimensions.

With the measurements in hand, an analysis comparing survey results and evaluations with metrics measurements can be undertaken. A 2 × 2 matrix representation of the comparison can be quite useful (see figure

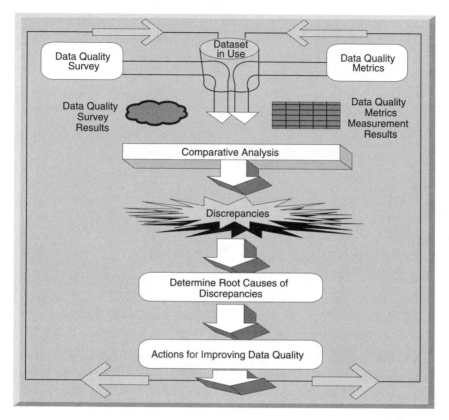

Figure 3.1
A Diagnostic Approach: Overview
Source: Adapted from Pipino, Lee, and Wang, 2002, p. 216.

3.2). The outcome of the analysis will fall in one of four quadrants. The goal is to achieve a data quality state that falls into quadrant IV. If the analysis indicates quadrant I, II, or III, then the company must investigate the root causes of discrepancies and take corrective actions. In each case corrective action will be different.

For example, if the metrics assessment of a dimension indicates data of high quality and the survey assessments indicate data of low quality (quadrant III), the reason for this conflict must be investigated. It is possible that in the past the quality of data was poor and that this view persists in the minds of the respondents even though the quality of data has indeed improved greatly and hence deserves the high objective rating. Alternatively, it may be that what is being measured objectively is not

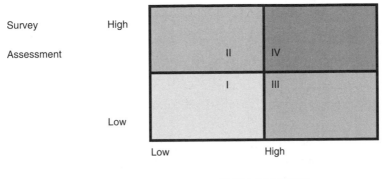

Figure 3.2
A Diagnostic Approach: Survey and Metrics Assessments
Source: Pipino, Lee, and Wang, 2002, p. 217.

quite what the stakeholder is evaluating and that there is a problem with the data or with what is being measured. Information of this type aids in the diagnosis of problems.

Obtaining Subjective Evaluations: The IQA Survey

The intent of the Information Quality Assessment (IQA) survey instrument (CRG, 1997a) is to obtain the respondents' subjective assessments of data quality and the respondents' knowledge of the data quality processes, programs, and tools that are in place. The respondents will consist of individuals whose interaction with organization's information is as a collector, a custodian, or a consumer.

The IQA questionnaire is constructed using a Likert-type scale ranging from 0 to 10, where 0 indicates "not at all" and 10 "completely." The survey is divided into eight sections. Section 1 ascertains the characteristics of the information source being assessed and which of the three roles (collector, custodian, consumer) the respondent represents. Managers of individuals performing a specific role are considered members of that role group. Section 2 of the IQA assesses the dimensional quality of the information. Section 3 of the IQA collects information about the respondent's knowledge regarding the data quality environment of the organization, including such considerations as knowledge of the existence of a data quality program, who is responsible for data quality, and what data quality software tools are employed. Section 4 collects background information regarding data quality problems. Sections 5, 6, and 7 collect information from the respondents on their knowledge (what, how, and why) of the collection, storage, and use processes. Section 8 collects the respondent's importance ratings of the data quality dimensions. A complete copy of the IQA appears in the appendix to this chapter.

The demographic information obtained from section 1 becomes quite useful in subsequent analyses and diagnoses. It provides a background and context for the information obtained in sections 2–8. It is useful to have when performing comparison evaluations across roles and across databases. Having the information from sections 2–8 enhances any analyses and diagnoses. All this information would be part of the input to the comparative analysis, the determination of root causes, and the resolution of discrepancies.

To make it easier to complete the questionnaire, an electronic version of the IQA has been created. Both the paper version and the electronic version have been used by numerous organizations. It is preferable to use the electronic version because this allows the direct capture of answers. It is axiomatic that the most accurate assessment will occur and errors will be minimized if the answers are captured directly from the source of the information, that is, the respondent. Transformations by intermediaries can introduce errors. The examples shown in figures 3.3 and 3.4 are screen shots of the electronic version of the IQA survey.

The first 16 questions of the full complement of 69 questions of section 2 are shown in figure 3.4. The subject responds to questions by selecting the appropriate numerical response from 0 to 10. The response that the subject has chosen is displayed to the left of the selection buttons. If the subject wishes, the responses can be typed in directly in the box to the left of the button.

The questionnaire has been used effectively by a number of Fortune 500 firms and also by agencies in the public sector. Administering the questionnaire provides the basis on which to analyze the state of data quality as perceived by each of the stakeholder groups. Comparative analyses across the groups can be performed. The relative importance of different dimensions to each of the stakeholders will also be available. The organization can benchmark its information quality assessments against a best-practice organization. These analyses help organizations focus their improvement efforts on assessment. All this information can

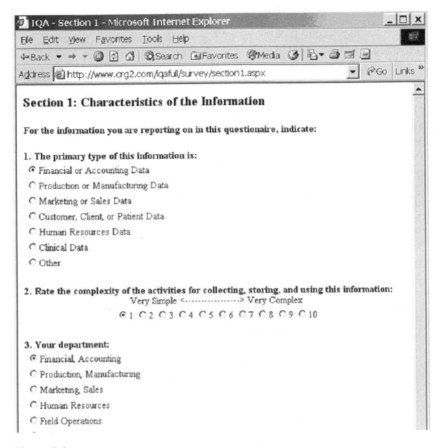

Figure 3.3
Sample Section 1 of Information Quality Assessment (IQA) Survey
Source: Cambridge Research Group (CRG, 1997a).

then be used and compared with the objective measurements to enrich the diagnostic approach. An example of the type of analysis that can result is shown in figure 3.5, which graphs the subjective assessments of information quality across the three stakeholder roles.

It is evident that there is some difference of opinion across stakeholders with respect to the quality of data along some of the dimensions. Figure 3.5 shows that three of the stakeholders are somewhat in agreement that the quality is reasonably good, whereas the manager rates the quality lower. Similarly, on dimension 14 there is a difference in ratings between the information custodian, the manager, and the collector.

IQA - Section 2 - Microsoft Internet Explorer

File Edit View Favorites Tools Help

Back ▼ → ▼ ⊗ 🖾 🏠 | Search Favorites Media | 🖾▼ 🖶 🗐 📄   Links »

Section 2: Information Quality Assessment

For each statement, indicate the extent to which it is true of this information. "This information" refers to the information or database selected by your company for reporting on in this information quality questionnaire	Not at all <------> Completely											
	0	1	2	3	4	5	6	7	8	9	10	
This information is easy to manipulate to meet our needs.	○	○	○	○	○	○	○	○	○	○	○	⊙
It is easy to interpret what this information means	○	○	○	○	○	○	○	○	○	○	○	⊙
This information is consistently presented in the same format.	○	○	○	○	○	○	○	○	○	○	○	⊙
This information includes all necessary values.	○	○	○	○	○	○	○	○	○	○	○	⊙
This information is easily retrievable.	○	○	○	○	○	○	○	○	○	○	○	⊙
This information is formatted compactly.	○	○	○	○	○	○	○	○	○	○	○	⊙
This information is protected against unauthorized access.	○	○	○	○	○	○	○	○	○	○	○	⊙
This information is incomplete.	○	○	○	○	○	○	○	○	○	○	○	⊙
This information is not presented consistently.	○	○	○	○	○	○	○	○	○	○	○	⊙
This information has a poor reputation for quality.	○	○	○	○	○	○	○	○	○	○	○	⊙
This information is complete.	○	○	○	○	○	○	○	○	○	○	○	⊙
This information is presented concisely.	○	○	○	○	○	○	○	○	○	○	○	⊙
This information is easy to understand.	○	○	○	○	○	○	○	○	○	○	○	⊙
This information is believable.	○	○	○	○	○	○	○	○	○	○	○	⊙
This information is easy to aggregate.	○	○	○	○	○	○	○	○	○	○	○	⊙
This information is of sufficient volume for our needs.	○	○	○	○	○	○	○	○	○	○	○	⊙

Done   Internet

Figure 3.4
Sample Section 2 of Information Quality Assessment (IQA) Survey
Source: Cambridge Research Group (CRG, 1997a).

Other analyses could compare the importance ratings given each of the data quality dimensions by the different stakeholders. Further, these importance ratings could be combined with the quality ratings to obtain a quality rating weighted by importance ratings. Although statistically such a combination may be theoretically questionable, it may serve a practical purpose by not giving excessive weight to dimensions that are of less importance to the firm.

Gap Analysis Techniques

The IQA questionnaire permits assessment of information quality at the dimension level. This can be done, for example, to examine how the organization compares to other competing organizations (benchmarking) or to compare responses from individuals filling different roles in the organization. This leads to the two techniques of benchmark gap analysis

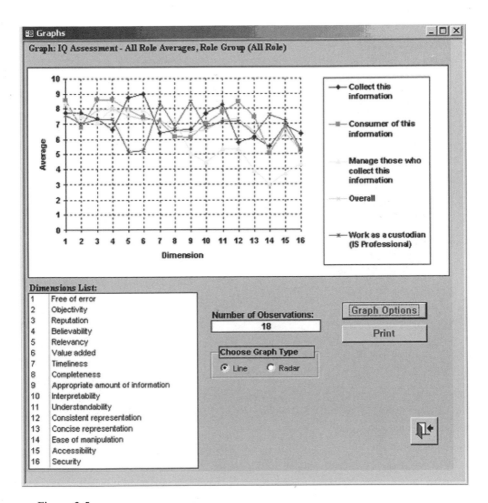

Figure 3.5
Information Quality Assessment across Roles
Source: Huang, Lee, and Wang, 1999.

and role gap analysis, both of which are useful in identifying information quality problem areas (Lee et al., 2002).

Benchmark Gap Analysis

A common concern in organizations is how well they are doing relative to others. Benchmarking addresses this concern. The IQA questionnaire provides a method of establishing the state of information quality in an organization at any given time. For best-practice organizations, the IQA

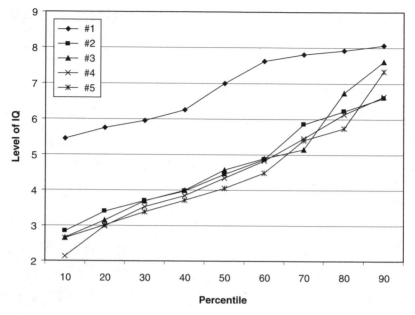

Figure 3.6
Benchmark Gap Example for "Data Are Easy to Use"
Source: Lee et al., 2002, p. 141.

measurement represents a benchmark against which other organizations can assess data quality.

The first technique, benchmark gap analysis, assesses an organization's information quality against a benchmark. Figure 3.6 shows a simplified benchmark gap diagram for the ease-of-use dimension ("Data are easy to use"), comparing four different companies with the benchmark company #1. The y-axis is the level of quality, which can range from 0 to 10. The x-axis is the percentage of respondents who rated the quality as being at that level.

When analyzing benchmark gaps, three indicators should be considered:

• Size of the gap area
• Location of the gap
• Different-sized gaps over the x-axis

There is a substantial gap between the best-practice organization and the four other organizations. Thus there is room for greatly improving the

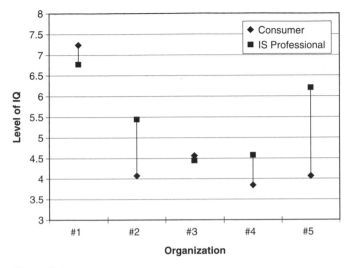

Figure 3.7
Role Gap Example for "Data Are Easy to Use"
Source: Lee et al., 2002, p. 142.

usability of data in all four organizations. The location of the gap refers to its placement on the *y*-axis. For example, at 10 percent the gap is located between 2 and 5.5, whereas at 60 percent the gap is located between 4.5 and 7.6. In this case, the size of the gap does not change much for different values of the *x*-axis. For company 3, however, the size of the gap is smaller after the 70th percentile.

Role Gap Analysis
Role gap analysis compares data quality assessments from respondents in different organization roles, information systems professionals, and information consumers. Role gap analysis is a useful diagnostic technique for determining whether differences between roles are a source of a benchmark gap. The assessment and comparison across roles serves to identify information quality problems and lays the foundation for improving them.

Figure 3.7 shows a simplified role gap diagram for the ease-of-use dimension. Each discrete point along the *x*-axis represents one of five organizations. Organization 1 is the best-practice organization. The numerical identifiers of the organizations are the same as those used in figure 3.6. The *y*-axis is the level of quality. The points in the figure 3.7

graph are the mean levels of information quality reported by information consumers and information systems professionals. The line between the diamond and the square for each organization represents the size of the role gap.

When analyzing role gaps, three indicators should be considered:

• Size of the gap area
• Location of the gap
• Direction of the gap (positive or negative)

In figure 3.7 the size of the role gap (the length of the line) is noticeably greater for organizations 2 and 5 than for organizations 3 and 4, which means that in the former two companies, information consumers and professionals disagreed substantially about how easy it is to use the data in the company's system. The location of the gap for the best-practice organization is approximately at 7, which is quite good. In contrast, the location of the gap for company 3 is about 4.5. Although the sizes of the two organizations are similar, organization 1 had much better information quality than organization 3. The direction of the gap is defined to be positive when information systems professionals assess the level of data quality to be higher than information consumers do. Thus organization 5 had a large positive gap. The best-practice organization had a small negative gap.

A large positive gap means that the professionals are not aware of problems that information consumers are experiencing. In general, organizations with a large positive gap should focus on reducing the problem by gaining consensus between information professionals and consumers. If the size of the gap is small, organizations are positioned to improve the quality of their information because they have consensus about its level. If the size of the gap is small, then the location of the gap should be examined. If it is high, indicating high information quality, incremental improvements are most appropriate, whereas if it is low, major improvement efforts have the potential for significant quality improvement.

Data Integrity Assessment

A third technique for the assessment of data quality is the process-embedded data integrity approach. Data integrity rules are assessed in conjunction with the process-oriented Total Data Quality Management cycle.

To ensure that data integrity rules reflect the dynamic, global nature of real-world states, organizations need a process that guides the mapping of changing real-world states into redefined data integrity rules. One solution is to embed data integrity rules into the TDQM process (CRG 1997b), producing the following steps for improving data quality. An organization first defines what data quality means for its data and context, producing data integrity rules. Next, it measures the quality of data against these integrity rules. Measurement may involve simple metrics, such as the percentage of violations, or more elaborate metrics, such as the difference between the data and the defined data quality standard. Third, the underlying causes of violations are analyzed, producing a plan to improve the quality of data to conform to data integrity rules. In addition, data integrity rules are redefined when purported violations are actually valid data. This redefinition operation is of the utmost importance for the continual improvement of data quality and makes the process more than simply iterative.

The result is process-embedded data integrity, in which the use of data integrity tools is explicitly linked to organization processes for improving data quality in the context of global and dynamic data changes. It serves as a potent means of making the organization's data integrity rules more visible and identifiable. It promotes reflection on the rules and facilitates communicating them throughout the organization. The consequence is support for the dynamic and global nature of organization data. This technique and a specific data integrity tool are addressed at greater length in chapter 4.

Concluding Remarks

In this chapter we introduced the concept of subjective evaluations of data quality from the perspective of each of the stakeholders—collector, custodian, and consumer. This is an important factor in increasing data quality awareness in the organization. In addition, we presented a diagnostic procedure and a comparative analysis procedure that can be used to improve data quality. As part of these procedures, one needs subjective evaluations of data quality. One of the tools used to obtain the subjective assessments is the Information Quality Assessment (IQA) survey. This tool has been automated and used extensively.

Numerous and varied analyses can be conducted with the information provided by such an instrument. Properly applied, the methods discussed in this chapter can form an effective methodology for assessing information quality in various organization settings where decisions must be made to prioritize tasks and allocate resources for improvement.

In the next chapter objective measures of data quality dimensions are discussed. These are required in order to conduct the necessary comparisons with the subjective assessments as part of the diagnostic procedure.

Appendix: Information Quality Assessment (IQA) Survey

More information and customized versions of the IQA survey are available from ⟨info@crg2.com⟩.

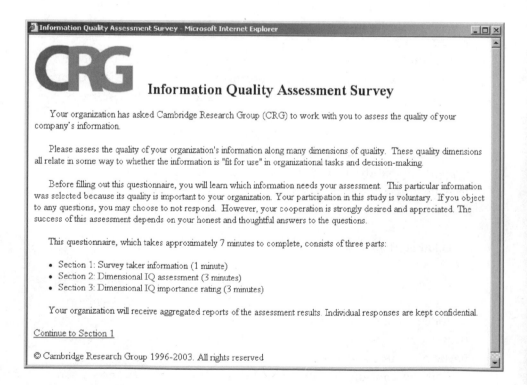

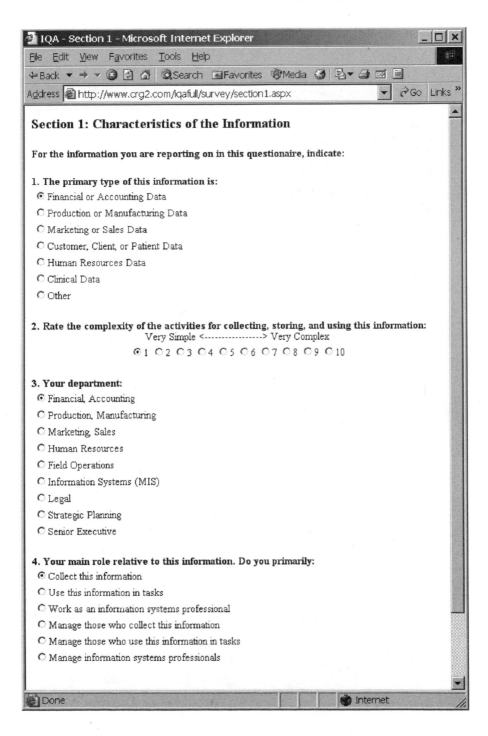

IQA - Section 1 - Microsoft Internet Explorer

File Edit View Favorites Tools Help

←Back ▾ → ▾ ⊗ ⊡ ⌂ | ⬤Search ⬛Favorites ⬤Media ⬤ | ⬤▾ ⬤ ⬤ ⬤

Address http://www.crg2.com/iqafull/survey/section1.aspx ▾ ⬤Go Links »

Section 1: Characteristics of the Information

For the information you are reporting on in this questionaire, indicate:

1. The primary type of this information is:

⦿ Financial or Accounting Data

○ Production or Manufacturing Data

○ Marketing or Sales Data

○ Customer, Client, or Patient Data

○ Human Resources Data

○ Clinical Data

○ Other

2. Rate the complexity of the activities for collecting, storing, and using this information:

Very Simple <----------------> Very Complex

⦿ 1 ○ 2 ○ 3 ○ 4 ○ 5 ○ 6 ○ 7 ○ 8 ○ 9 ○ 10

3. Your department:

⦿ Financial, Accounting

○ Production, Manufacturing

○ Marketing, Sales

○ Human Resources

○ Field Operations

○ Information Systems (MIS)

○ Legal

○ Strategic Planning

○ Senior Executive

4. Your main role relative to this information. Do you primarily:

⦿ Collect this information

○ Use this information in tasks

○ Work as an information systems professional

○ Manage those who collect this information

○ Manage those who use this information in tasks

○ Manage information systems professionals

Done   Internet

IQA - Section 2 - Microsoft Internet Explorer   _ □ ×

File   Edit   View   Favorites   Tools   Help

← Back ▼ → ▼ ⊗ ⊡ ⚷ | ⊘Search ⊞Favorites ⊕Media ⊗ | ⊑▼ ⊜ ⊠ ⊟   Links »

Section 2: Information Quality Assessment

For each statement, indicate the extent to which it is true of this information. "This information" refers to the information or database selected by your company for reporting on in this information quality questionnaire	Not at all <------> Completely											
	0	1	2	3	4	5	6	7	8	9	10	
This information is easy to manipulate to meet our needs.	○	○	○	○	○	○	○	○	○	○	○	⊙
It is easy to interpret what this information means.	○	○	○	○	○	○	○	○	○	○	○	⊙
This information is consistently presented in the same format.	○	○	○	○	○	○	○	○	○	○	○	⊙
This information includes all necessary values.	○	○	○	○	○	○	○	○	○	○	○	⊙
This information is easily retrievable.	○	○	○	○	○	○	○	○	○	○	○	⊙
This information is formatted compactly.	○	○	○	○	○	○	○	○	○	○	○	⊙
This information is protected against unauthorized access.	○	○	○	○	○	○	○	○	○	○	○	⊙
This information is incomplete.	○	○	○	○	○	○	○	○	○	○	○	⊙
This information is not presented consistently.	○	○	○	○	○	○	○	○	○	○	○	⊙
This information has a poor reputation for quality.	○	○	○	○	○	○	○	○	○	○	○	⊙
This information is complete.	○	○	○	○	○	○	○	○	○	○	○	⊙
This information is presented concisely.	○	○	○	○	○	○	○	○	○	○	○	⊙
This information is easy to understand.	○	○	○	○	○	○	○	○	○	○	○	⊙
This information is believable.	○	○	○	○	○	○	○	○	○	○	○	⊙
This information is easy to aggregate.	○	○	○	○	○	○	○	○	○	○	○	⊙
This information is of sufficient volume for our needs.	○	○	○	○	○	○	○	○	○	○	○	⊙
This information is correct.	○	○	○	○	○	○	○	○	○	○	○	⊙
This information is useful to our work.	○	○	○	○	○	○	○	○	○	○	○	⊙
This information provides a major benefit to our work.	○	○	○	○	○	○	○	○	○	○	○	⊙
This information is easily accessible.	○	○	○	○	○	○	○	○	○	○	○	⊙
This information has a good reputation.	○	○	○	○	○	○	○	○	○	○	○	⊙
This information is sufficiently current for our work.	○	○	○	○	○	○	○	○	○	○	○	⊙
This information is difficult to interpret.	○	○	○	○	○	○	○	○	○	○	○	⊙
This information is not protected with adequate security.	○	○	○	○	○	○	○	○	○	○	○	⊙
This information is of doubtful credibility.	○	○	○	○	○	○	○	○	○	○	○	⊙
The amount of information does not match our needs.	○	○	○	○	○	○	○	○	○	○	○	⊙
This information is difficult to manipulate to meet our needs.	○	○	○	○	○	○	○	○	○	○	○	⊙
This information is not sufficiently timely.	○	○	○	○	○	○	○	○	○	○	○	⊙

⊘ Done   ⊕ Internet

IQA - Section 2 - Microsoft Internet Explorer

File   Edit   View   Favorites   Tools   Help

Back ▼ → ▼ ⊗ ⊠ ⌂ | Search ⊞Favorites ⊛Media ⊛ | ⊠▼ ⊜ ⊟ ⊟   Links »

This information is not sufficiently timely.	○	○	○	○	○	○	○	○	○	○	○	◉
This information is difficult to aggregate.	○	○	○	○	○	○	○	○	○	○	○	◉
The amount of information is not sufficient for our needs.	○	○	○	○	○	○	○	○	○	○	○	◉
This information is incorrect.	○	○	○	○	○	○	○	○	○	○	○	◉
This information does not add value to our work.	○	○	○	○	○	○	○	○	○	○	○	◉
This information was objectively collected.	○	○	○	○	○	○	○	○	○	○	○	◉
It is difficult to interpret the coded information.	○	○	○	○	○	○	○	○	○	○	○	◉
The meaning of this information is difficult to understand.	○	○	○	○	○	○	○	○	○	○	○	◉
This information is not sufficiently current for our work.	○	○	○	○	○	○	○	○	○	○	○	◉
This information is easily interpretable.	○	○	○	○	○	○	○	○	○	○	○	◉
The amount of information is neither too much nor too little.	○	○	○	○	○	○	○	○	○	○	○	◉
This information is accurate.	○	○	○	○	○	○	○	○	○	○	○	◉
Access to this information is sufficiently restricted.	○	○	○	○	○	○	○	○	○	○	○	◉
This information is presented consistently.	○	○	○	○	○	○	○	○	○	○	○	◉
This information has a reputation for quality.	○	○	○	○	○	○	○	○	○	○	○	◉
This information is easy to comprehend.	○	○	○	○	○	○	○	○	○	○	○	◉
This information is based on facts.	○	○	○	○	○	○	○	○	○	○	○	◉
This information is sufficiently complete for our needs.	○	○	○	○	○	○	○	○	○	○	○	◉
This information is trustworthy.	○	○	○	○	○	○	○	○	○	○	○	◉
This information is relevant to our work.	○	○	○	○	○	○	○	○	○	○	○	◉
Using this information increases the value of our work.	○	○	○	○	○	○	○	○	○	○	○	◉
This information is presented in a compact form.	○	○	○	○	○	○	○	○	○	○	○	◉
This information is appropriate for our work.	○	○	○	○	○	○	○	○	○	○	○	◉
The meaning of this information is easy to understand.	○	○	○	○	○	○	○	○	○	○	○	◉
This information is credible.	○	○	○	○	○	○	○	○	○	○	○	◉
This information covers the needs of our tasks.	○	○	○	○	○	○	○	○	○	○	○	◉
The representation of this information is compact and concise.	○	○	○	○	○	○	○	○	○	○	○	◉
This information adds value to our tasks.	○	○	○	○	○	○	○	○	○	○	○	◉
The measurement units for this information are clear.	○	○	○	○	○	○	○	○	○	○	○	◉
This information is objective.	○	○	○	○	○	○	○	○	○	○	○	◉
This information can only be accessed by people who should see it.	○	○	○	○	○	○	○	○	○	○	○	◉
This information is sufficiently timely.	○	○	○	○	○	○	○	○	○	○	○	◉

Done   Internet

IQA - Section 2 - Microsoft Internet Explorer											

File Edit View Favorites Tools Help

← Back ▾ → ▾ ⊗ 🕑 ⌂ | 🔍Search ⭐Favorites 🎬Media 🎦 | 🔄▾ 🖨 📝 📄 Links »

This information is sufficiently timely.	○	○	○	○	○	○	○	○	○	○	⊙
This information is easy to combine with other information.	○	○	○	○	○	○	○	○	○	○	⊙
This information is represented in a consistent format.	○	○	○	○	○	○	○	○	○	○	⊙
This information is easily obtainable.	○	○	○	○	○	○	○	○	○	○	⊙
This information comes from good sources.	○	○	○	○	○	○	○	○	○	○	⊙
This information is quickly accessible when needed.	○	○	○	○	○	○	○	○	○	○	⊙
This information has sufficient breadth and depth for our tasks.	○	○	○	○	○	○	○	○	○	○	⊙
This information presents an impartial view.	○	○	○	○	○	○	○	○	○	○	⊙
This information is applicable to our work.	○	○	○	○	○	○	○	○	○	○	⊙
This information is sufficiently up-to-date for our work.	○	○	○	○	○	○	○	○	○	○	⊙
This information is reliable.	○	○	○	○	○	○	○	○	○	○	⊙

Back to section 1	Reset	Save	Save and continue to section 3

Note: Save your data before continuing to another section.

🔵 Done   🌐 Internet

IQA - Section 3 - Microsoft Internet Explorer

File Edit View Favorites Tools Help

Back ▾ → ▾ ⊗ 🖹 🏠 🔍Search 📁Favorites 🕲Media 🕃 🖫▾ 🖨 🖃 🖹   Links »

Section 3: Information Quality Context Assessment

For each statement, indicate the extent to which it characterizes your organization and its quality activities.	Not at all <------> Completely											
	1	2	3	4	5	6	7	8	9	10	N/A	
This company has adopted a TQM approach.	○	○	○	○	○	○	○	○	○	○	○	◉
This company has tools that identify deficiencies with this information.	○	○	○	○	○	○	○	○	○	○	○	◉
In this company, there are people whose primary job is to assure the quality of information.	○	○	○	○	○	○	○	○	○	○	○	◉
This company has tools to assure the consistency of this information.	○	○	○	○	○	○	○	○	○	○	○	◉
In this company, employees view continuous quality improvement as a part of their job.	○	○	○	○	○	○	○	○	○	○	○	◉
This company uses TQM to control process quality.	○	○	○	○	○	○	○	○	○	○	○	◉
This company has a specific position or group responsible for information quality.	○	○	○	○	○	○	○	○	○	○	○	◉
This company solves quality problems using one of the popular quality improvement methods such as one developed by Deming, Juran, or Crosby.	○	○	○	○	○	○	○	○	○	○	○	◉
In this company, there are designated people whose job is to solve information quality problems.	○	○	○	○	○	○	○	○	○	○	○	◉
This company has tools to assure the completeness of this information.	○	○	○	○	○	○	○	○	○	○	○	◉
In this company, there are designated people who are responsible for the quality of information.	○	○	○	○	○	○	○	○	○	○	○	◉
In this company, employees participate in quality improvement activities.	○	○	○	○	○	○	○	○	○	○	○	◉
This company has tools to assure the correctness of this information.	○	○	○	○	○	○	○	○	○	○	○	◉
This company provides software for aggregating, manipulating and summarizing this information.	○	○	○	○	○	○	○	○	○	○	○	◉
This company is developing a data dictionary to standardize data definitions across different computers or divisions.	○	○	○	○	○	○	○	○	○	○	○	◉
In this company, employees are able to take actions to improve the quality of information.	○	○	○	○	○	○	○	○	○	○	○	◉
This company has recently moved this information to a different hardware or software system.	○	○	○	○	○	○	○	○	○	○	○	◉
In this company, ensuring the quality of this information is the responsibility of those who use the information.	○	○	○	○	○	○	○	○	○	○	○	◉
This company has new (database) software for managing and storing this information.	○	○	○	○	○	○	○	○	○	○	○	◉
In this company, it is relatively easy to improve information as needed.	○	○	○	○	○	○	○	○	○	○	○	◉

Back to section 2	Reset	Save	Save and continue to section 4

Note: Save your data before continuing to another section.

Done   Internet

IQA - Section 4 - Microsoft Internet Explorer

File   Edit   View   Favorites   Tools   Help

Back ▾ → ▾ ⊗ ⊡ ⌂ | ⊚Search ⊞Favorites ⊛Media ⊛ ⊟▾ ⊜ ⊠ ⊟   Links »

Section 4: Background Information

4.1 Briefly explain the ways in which the information is important to your company:

4.2 Examples of Information Quality (IQ) problems:

4.2a Describe an IQ problem in your organization.

4.2b How was the problem discovered?

4.2c How was the problem solved?

4.2d Are there more appropriate or long-term solutions?

Done   Internet

IQA - Section 4 - Microsoft Internet Explorer — □ ×

File   Edit   View   Favorites   Tools   Help

⇐ Back ▾ ⇒ ▾ ⊗ ⬚ ⌂ | ⊘ Search ⬚ Favorites ⬚ Media ⬚ | ⬚ ▾ ⬚ ⬚ ⬚   Links »

4.3 Your background:

4.3a How long have you worked for this company?
- ⦿ Less than 1 year
- ○ 1 to 5 years
- ○ 6 to 10 years
- ○ Greater than 10 years

4.3b How many years of experience do you have?
- ⦿ Less than 1 year
- ○ 1 to 5 years
- ○ 6 to 10 years
- ○ Greater than 10 years

4.3c How long have you held your current job?
- ⦿ Less than 1 year
- ○ 1 to 5 years
- ○ 6 to 10 years
- ○ Greater than 10 years

4.3d Highest educational level or degree?
- ⦿ High School
- ○ Associate's Degree
- ○ College Degree
- ○ Graduate Degree

4.3e Gender?
- ⦿ Female
- ○ Male

| Back to section 3 | Reset | Save | Save and continue to section 5 |

Note: Save your data before continuing to another section.

Done   Internet

IQA - Section 5 - Microsoft Internet Explorer

File   Edit   View   Favorites   Tools   Help

← Back ▾ → ▾ ⊗ 🖹 🖄 | ⊗Search 🖃Favorites 🎲Media ⊗ | 🖺▾ 🖨 🖼 🖹   Links »

Section 5: Information Collection

For each statement, indicate the extent to which it is true about your knowledge of this information and its collection in your organization.	Not at all <------> Completely										
	1	2	3	4	5	6	7	8	9	10	
I know which group collects this information.	○	○	○	○	○	○	○	○	○	○	◉
I know how to fix routine problems with collecting this information.	○	○	○	○	○	○	○	○	○	○	◉
I know the sources of this information.	○	○	○	○	○	○	○	○	○	○	◉
I understand the information collection procedures well enough to recognize why this information is collected incorrectly.	○	○	○	○	○	○	○	○	○	○	◉
I know the usual solutions for problems with collecting this information.	○	○	○	○	○	○	○	○	○	○	◉
I know the problems encountered in collecting this information.	○	○	○	○	○	○	○	○	○	○	◉
I cannot find the causes of new problems in collecting this information.	○	○	○	○	○	○	○	○	○	○	◉
I do not know the sources of this information.	○	○	○	○	○	○	○	○	○	○	◉
I know why it is difficult to collect all this information.	○	○	○	○	○	○	○	○	○	○	◉
I know the standard procedures for correcting deficiencies in information when collecting it.	○	○	○	○	○	○	○	○	○	○	◉
I know who creates this information.	○	○	○	○	○	○	○	○	○	○	◉
I can detect sources of new problems in collecting this information.	○	○	○	○	○	○	○	○	○	○	◉
I know the steps taken to gather this information.	○	○	○	○	○	○	○	○	○	○	◉
When typical problems arise with collecting this information, I know how we handle them.	○	○	○	○	○	○	○	○	○	○	◉
I cannot diagnose why this collected information is deficient.	○	○	○	○	○	○	○	○	○	○	◉
I do not know the usual solutions for problems with collecting this information.	○	○	○	○	○	○	○	○	○	○	◉
I can recognize new problems as they arise in collecting this information.	○	○	○	○	○	○	○	○	○	○	◉
I do not know which group collects this information.	○	○	○	○	○	○	○	○	○	○	◉
I know how to fix recurring problems with collecting this information.	○	○	○	○	○	○	○	○	○	○	◉
I know the procedures by which this information is collected.	○	○	○	○	○	○	○	○	○	○	◉
I do not know how to fix routine problems with collecting this information.	○	○	○	○	○	○	○	○	○	○	◉

| Back to section 4 | Reset | Save | Save and continue to section 6 |

Done   Internet

```
IQA - Section 6 - Microsoft Internet Explorer                              _ □ x
File  Edit  View  Favorites  Tools  Help
⇐Back  ▼  ⇒  ▼  ⊘  ⬆  ⌂  | ⚲Search  ⬜Favorites  ⬢Media  ⬢  | ⬛▼ ⬛ ⬛ ⬛        Links »
```

Section 6: Information Storage

For each statement, indicate the extent to which it is true about your knowledge of this information and its storage in your organization.	Not at all <------> Completely										
	1	2	3	4	5	6	7	8	9	10	
I know the steps taken to store and maintain this information in our computers.	○	○	○	○	○	○	○	○	○	○	⊙
I know some of the problems in storing this information appropriately in our computers.	○	○	○	○	○	○	○	○	○	○	⊙
I know how to fix recurring problems with storing this information in our computers.	○	○	○	○	○	○	○	○	○	○	⊙
I know which group maintains this information in our computers.	○	○	○	○	○	○	○	○	○	○	⊙
I can recognize new problems as they arise in storing and maintaining this information in our computers.	○	○	○	○	○	○	○	○	○	○	⊙
When typical problems arise with storing this information in our computers, I know how we handle them.	○	○	○	○	○	○	○	○	○	○	⊙
I know which software is used for storing this information in our computers.	○	○	○	○	○	○	○	○	○	○	⊙
I do not know how to fix routine problems with storing this information in our computers.	○	○	○	○	○	○	○	○	○	○	⊙
I know the procedures used to store this information in our computers.	○	○	○	○	○	○	○	○	○	○	⊙
I know why people have difficulty with computer access procedures for this information.	○	○	○	○	○	○	○	○	○	○	⊙
I understand our computing environment well enough to analyze why this information is stored inadequately.	○	○	○	○	○	○	○	○	○	○	⊙
I know why it is difficult to store all this information in our computers.	○	○	○	○	○	○	○	○	○	○	⊙
I know how to fix routine problems with storing this information in our computers.	○	○	○	○	○	○	○	○	○	○	⊙
I know who maintains this information in our computers.	○	○	○	○	○	○	○	○	○	○	⊙
I know the usual solutions for problems with storing this information in our computers.	○	○	○	○	○	○	○	○	○	○	⊙
I know why it is difficult to store this information in our computers in an easy-to-interpret manner.	○	○	○	○	○	○	○	○	○	○	⊙
I do not know how to fix recurring problems with storing this information in our computers.	○	○	○	○	○	○	○	○	○	○	⊙
I do not know which group maintains this information in our computers.	○	○	○	○	○	○	○	○	○	○	⊙
I know our standard procedures for correcting deficiencies in information when storing it in our computers.	○	○	○	○	○	○	○	○	○	○	⊙
I know which of our computers stores this information.	○	○	○	○	○	○	○	○	○	○	⊙
I know why this information is displayed in this form in our computers.	○	○	○	○	○	○	○	○	○	○	⊙

| Back to section 5 | Reset | Save | Save and continue to section 7 |

Note: Save your data before continuing to another section.

```
⊞ Done                                               ● Internet
```

IQA - Section 7 - Microsoft Internet Explorer

File Edit View Favorites Tools Help

Back ▾ → ▾ ❌ 🔄 🏠 | Search Favorites Media | Links »

Section 7: Information Use

For each statement, indicate the extent to which it is true about your knowledge of this information and its use in your organization.	Not at all <------> Completely										
	1	2	3	4	5	6	7	8	9	10	
I know which group uses this information.	○	○	○	○	○	○	○	○	○	○	⦿
I know the usual solutions for problems with using this information.	○	○	○	○	○	○	○	○	○	○	⦿
I know the steps taken when using this information.	○	○	○	○	○	○	○	○	○	○	⦿
I do not know how to fix routine problems with using this information.	○	○	○	○	○	○	○	○	○	○	⦿
I can recognize new problems as they arise in using this information in a new task.	○	○	○	○	○	○	○	○	○	○	⦿
I can diagnose problems in using this information.	○	○	○	○	○	○	○	○	○	○	⦿
I know the tasks which require the use of this information.	○	○	○	○	○	○	○	○	○	○	⦿
I do not know our standard procedures for correcting deficiencies in information when using it.	○	○	○	○	○	○	○	○	○	○	⦿
I cannot find the causes of new problems in the use of this information.	○	○	○	○	○	○	○	○	○	○	⦿
I know the computer access procedures for obtaining this information.	○	○	○	○	○	○	○	○	○	○	⦿
I know some of the problems in ensuring that this information is used appropriately.	○	○	○	○	○	○	○	○	○	○	⦿
I know who (individual or group) uses this information.	○	○	○	○	○	○	○	○	○	○	⦿
When typical problems, such as interpretation or access, arise with using this information, I know how we handle them.	○	○	○	○	○	○	○	○	○	○	⦿
I cannot recognize when new problems arise in using this information in a new task.	○	○	○	○	○	○	○	○	○	○	⦿
I do not know how to fix recurring problems with using this information.	○	○	○	○	○	○	○	○	○	○	⦿
I know how to fix routine problems with using this information.	○	○	○	○	○	○	○	○	○	○	⦿
I know the procedures in which this information is used.	○	○	○	○	○	○	○	○	○	○	⦿
I do not know which group uses this information.	○	○	○	○	○	○	○	○	○	○	⦿
I can detect sources of new problems in using this information.	○	○	○	○	○	○	○	○	○	○	⦿
I know our standard procedures for correcting deficiencies in information when using it.	○	○	○	○	○	○	○	○	○	○	⦿

| Back to section 6 | Reset | Save | Save and continue to section 8 |

Note: Save your data before continuing to another section.

Done   Internet

Section 8: Importance Rating

For each dimension, indicate the importance level of this information. for use in your tasks.	Not at all <------> Completely										
	1	2	3	4	5	6	7	8	9	10	
Data is available, or easily and quickly retrievable	○	○	○	○	○	○	○	○	○	○	⊙
The volume of data is appropriate for the task at hand	○	○	○	○	○	○	○	○	○	○	⊙
Data is regarded as true and credible	○	○	○	○	○	○	○	○	○	○	⊙
Data is not missing and is of sufficient breadth and depth for the task at hand	○	○	○	○	○	○	○	○	○	○	⊙
Data is compactly represented	○	○	○	○	○	○	○	○	○	○	⊙
Data is presented in the same format	○	○	○	○	○	○	○	○	○	○	⊙
Data is easy to manipulate and apply to different tasks	○	○	○	○	○	○	○	○	○	○	⊙
Data is correct and reliable	○	○	○	○	○	○	○	○	○	○	⊙
Data is in appropriate languages, symbols, and units, and the definitions are clear	○	○	○	○	○	○	○	○	○	○	⊙
Data is unbiased, unprejudiced, and impartial	○	○	○	○	○	○	○	○	○	○	⊙
Data is applicable and helpful for the task at hand	○	○	○	○	○	○	○	○	○	○	⊙
Data is highly regarded in terms of its source or content	○	○	○	○	○	○	○	○	○	○	⊙
Access to data is restricted appropriately to maintain its security	○	○	○	○	○	○	○	○	○	○	⊙
Data is sufficiently up-to-date for the task at hand	○	○	○	○	○	○	○	○	○	○	⊙
Data is easily comprehended	○	○	○	○	○	○	○	○	○	○	⊙
Data is beneficial and provides advantages from its use	○	○	○	○	○	○	○	○	○	○	⊙

Back to section 7	Reset	Save	Save and finish

Note: Save your data before continuing to another section.

Source: CRG, 1997a.

4

Assessing Data Quality, Part II

Quantifiable measurements of specific data quality variables must be performed. These will be used in the diagnostic approach in which the subjective survey evaluations are compared to the quantitative metrics. In this chapter we focus on these quantitative metrics. When developing these measures, the company must determine what is to be measured: that set of data quality dimensions that are important to its mission and operations. Each organization must examine its operations and make its own determination.

We use the traditional database integrity constraints proposed by Codd (1970) and a subset of data quality dimensions (Wand and Wang 1996; Wang and Strong 1996) as the basis for our discussion of data quality metrics. We hope that the metrics discussed here will be usable of and in themselves and also serve as a basis on which the reader can develop new metrics to fit the organization's needs. Many of the formulations presented here are symbolic representations of metrics suggested by Pipino, Lee, and Wang (2002).

Codd Integrity Constraints

The Codd integrity constraints consist of entity integrity, referential integrity, domain integrity, and column integrity. Codd introduced a fifth, all-purpose category that he labeled business rules. This category is intended to capture integrity rules specific to an organization. The metrics developed to measure adherence to Codd's first four integrity constraints can be viewed as task-independent metrics. They reflect the states of the data without the contextual knowledge of the application.

They can be applied to any set of data regardless of the task or application at hand.

Entity integrity requires that no primary key field value in a table be null. A metric that reflects the degree of adherence to this rule can be the following:

Degree of adherence to entity integrity = 1 − (*Number of null primary keys/Total number of rows*)

The referential integrity rule states that the value of a foreign key in a table must match a value of a primary key in a designated related table, or the value of the foreign key must be null. Similar to the previous metric, a measure of adherence to the referential integrity rule would be

Degree of adherence to reference integrity = 1 − (*Number of nonmatching values excluding nulls in the dependent table/Total rows in the dependent table*)

Metrics for column integrity can be represented in a similar fashion. Column integrity requires that the values in the column be drawn from the set of permissible values. Again, a simple ratio reflecting the percentage of rows that adhere to this rule can be used:

Degree of adherence to column integrity = 1 − (*Number of invalid column values/Number of rows in table*)

Note that the preceding metrics are simple ratios and adhere to the following general form:

$$Rating = 1 - \left(\frac{Number\ of\ undesirable\ outcomes}{Total\ outcomes} \right)$$

The form follows the convention that 1 represents the most desirable and 0 the least desirable score. Typically, individuals are inclined to count exceptions to the rule rather than conformance with the rule. In addition, one would expect few exceptions, thus making the tabulation easier. The metric, however, should reflect the degree of adherence. Hence, for most metrics that are simple ratios, we suggest using the canonical form. In what follows, we extend our discussion to other useful dimensions and suggested metrics for their assessment.

Metrics for Data Quality

Basic Forms

Assessment of data quality requires assessments along a number of dimensions. Each organization must determine which of these dimensions are important to its operations and precisely define the variables that constitute the dimensions. These are the variables that will be measured. Many of the dimensions are multivariate in nature. Which variables are important to the firm must be clearly identified and defined.

Choosing the specific variables to measure can be much more difficult than defining the specific metric, which often reduces to the ratio form. In addition, many of these variables are context-dependent. Although falling within a specific dimensional category, the specific measure to assess a specific dimension will vary from organization to organization.

We examine a number of dimensions that can be used to assess data quality. We have chosen to discuss a set of dimensions that have been shown to be of particular interest and importance to many organizations.

Free of Error   It is a common practice to use the term *accuracy* when referring to whether the data is correct. The dimension of accuracy itself, however, can consist of one or more variables, only one of which is whether the data are correct. We use *free of error* to label the dimension that represents whether the data is correct. If one is counting the number of data units in error, then the metric is

$$\textit{Free-of-error rating} = 1 - \left(\frac{\textit{Number of data units in error}}{\textit{Total number of data units}} \right)$$

This formulation requires additional refinements. It certainly will require additional specificity based on context. A concise description of what constitutes a data unit is required. Is it a field, a record, a table? Further, what exactly constitutes an error? The sense of the precision of the measurement must be specified. Quite possibly, in one case an incorrect character in a text string is tolerable, whereas in another circumstance all characters must be correct. These are distinctions that make the metric context-dependent and that demand unambiguous definition. We cannot stress enough the importance of developing definitions that span databases and stakeholders.

Completeness   Another useful dimension is the completeness of the data. The completeness dimension can be viewed from at least three perspectives: schema completeness, column completeness, and population completeness. By schema completeness, we mean the degree to which entities and attributes are not missing from the schema. By column completeness, we mean the degree to which there exist missing values in a column of a table. Codd's column integrity, described earlier, can be considered a check of column completeness in the instance when a column represents a required property of an object. By population completeness, we mean the degree to which members of the population that should be present are not present. For example, if a column should contain at least one occurrence of all 50 states, but the column contains only 43 states, then the population is incomplete.

Each of the completeness types can be measured by the following simple ratio:

$$Completeness\ rating = 1 - \left(\frac{Number\ of\ incomplete\ items}{Total\ number\ of\ items} \right)$$

Consistency   The dimension of consistency can also be viewed from a number of perspectives. For example, one can be concerned with the consistency of redundant data in one table or in multiple tables. Codd's referential integrity constraint is an instantiation of this type of consistency. A second type would be the consistency between two related data elements. For example, the name of the city and the postal code should be consistent. This can be enabled by entering just the postal code and filling in the name of the city systematically through the use of referential integrity with a postal code table. A third form of consistency focuses on consistency of format for the same data element used in different tables. This may or may not be a requirement and will depend on context. The metric to measure any of these variables could take the following form:

$Consistency\ rating$

$$= 1 - \left(\frac{Number\ of\ instances\ violating\ specific\ consistency\ type}{Total\ number\ of\ consistency\ checks\ performed} \right)$$

Aggregate Forms

In the previous section, different types of completeness and consistency were discussed. It may be necessary to assess each category of the dimension and then generate an aggregate. In this case the values of *n* single variable metrics must be aggregated.

To handle dimensions that require the aggregation of multiple data quality indicators (variables), the minimum or maximum operation can be applied. The argument would consist of the individual data quality indicators for the multivariate dimension. The min operator is conservative in that it assigns to the dimension an aggregate value no higher than the value of its weakest data quality indicator (evaluated and normalized to between 0 and 1). The individual variables may be measured using a simple ratio. The maximum operation would be used if a liberal interpretation is warranted.

Let M_i represent the normalized value of the *i*th variable. Then the metric, using the min operator, takes the form $\min(M_1, M_2, \ldots, M_n)$, where $M_1, M_2, \ldots, M_n$ are normalized assessments of the variables of the dimension. The max operation takes the form $\max(M_1, M_2, \ldots, M_n)$, where $M_1, M_2, \ldots, M_n$ are normalized assessments of the variables of the dimension.

An alternative to the min operator is a weighted average of variables. For example, if a company has a good understanding of the importance of each variable to the overall evaluation of a dimension, then a weighted average of the variables would be appropriate. Formally, we would have

$$Rating = \sum_{i=1}^{n} a_i M_i$$

where a_i is a weighting factor, $0 \leq a_i \leq 1$, and $a_1 + a_2 + \cdots + a_n = 1$. M_i is a normalized value of the assessments of the *i*th variable.

Two examples of dimensions that can make use of the min operator are believability and appropriate amount of data.

Believability   Believability is the extent to which data is regarded as true and credible. As a rating of believability, one could use the subjective rating obtained as part of the IQA survey described in chapter 3. Alternatively, one might wish to define believability as a function of multiple variables. In this latter case either the min operation or the weighted average might be used to arrive at an aggregate rating. For example, believability may reflect an individual's assessment of the credibility of the source of the data, the perceived timeliness of the data, or assessment against a common standard. One might define believability as follows:

Believability = min(*Believability of source, Believability when compared to internal commonsense standard, Believability based on age of data*)

Each of these variables would be rated on a scale from 0 to 1. The overall believability would then be assigned as the minimum value of the three. Assume that the believability of the source is rated 0.6, on a commonsense standard is rated 0.8, and on age is rated 0.7; then the overall believability rating would be $\min(0.6, 0.8, 0.7) = 0.6$.

One must beware of using a weighted average for a dimension such as believability. It is easy to assume that one is dealing with interval data and to subject the data to operations that are appropriate for interval or ratio scale data. If in fact one is dealing with ordinal data, the manipulations are not appropriate, and the numerical results could lead to misinterpretation.

Appropriate Amount of Data   The min operator can also be used to calculate a measure for the appropriate amount of data. A working definition of the appropriate amount of data should reflect the state that the amount of data is neither too little nor too much. A metric would be

Rating of appropriate amount of data

$$= \min \left[\frac{Number\ of\ data\ units\ provided}{Number\ of\ data\ units\ needed}, \frac{Number\ of\ data\ units\ needed}{Number\ of\ data\ units\ provided} \right]$$

Complex Forms

Two dimensions of particular importance in practice are timeliness and accessibility. The metrics to measure these dimensions can be quite straightforward or can be modeled using a more complex formulation. We examine each briefly.

Timeliness   The timeliness dimension reflects how up-to-date the data is with respect to the task for which it is used. A general metric to measure timeliness has been proposed by Ballou et al. (1998):

$$Timeliness\ rating = \left\{ \max\left[\left(1 - \frac{Currency}{Volatility} \right), 0 \right] \right\}^{s}$$

where currency = (delivery time − input time) + age, volatility refers to the length of time over which the data remains valid, delivery time refers to the time at which the data was delivered to the user, input time refers to the time at which the data was received by the system, and age refers to the age of the data when it was first received by the system. The exponent's value is task-dependent. It allows one to control the sensitivity of timeliness to the ratio. For example, notice the rating is 0.81 without a sensitivity adjustment ($s = 1$), 0.49 when $s = 2$ (more sensitive and thereby becomes less timely faster), and 0.9 when $s = 0.5$ (less sensitive).

For some organizations, such a complex measure is not necessary. For example, the age of the data may be an adequate measure of timeliness. Again these metrics are dependent on the context in which they will be applied.

Accessibility   The accessibility dimension reflects the ease of attainability of the data. A metric that emphasizes the time aspect of accessibility can be defined as follows:

$$Accessibility\ rating = \left\{ \max\right.$$

$$\left. \cdot \left[\left(1 - \frac{Interval\ of\ time\ from\ request\ by\ user\ to\ delivery\ to\ user}{Interval\ of\ time\ from\ request\ to\ time\ at\ which\ no\ longer\ of\ any\ use} \right), 0 \right] \right\}^{s}$$

If the data is delivered just prior to the time at which it is no longer of use, it may be of some use but not as useful as if it had been delivered much earlier. This metric trades off the time interval over which the user needs the data against the amount of time it takes to deliver the data. Here the time to obtain data increases until the first term goes negative, at which time accessibility is rated zero.

The metric uses time as the basic measure of accessibility. One can also define accessibility based on the structure and relations of the data paths and path lengths in other applications. As always, if time, structure, and path lengths all are considered important, then individual metrics for each can be developed, and an overall measure using the min operator can be defined.

The general form of the foregoing complex metrics makes use of the max operator. The general form is as follows:

$$Rating = \left\{ \max\left[\left(1 - \frac{Variable\ 1}{Variable\ 2}\right), 0\right]\right\}^{s}$$

This form is useful when the dimension is a function of two variables, each of which participates in a trade-off. The exponent s is a sensitivity parameter.

Automating the Metrics

An outgrowth of MIT's Total Data Quality Management Research Program, the Integrity Analyzer (CRG 1997b) combines a TDQM methodology of define, measure, analyze, and improve with Codd's database integrity constraints of domain, entity, referential, column, and user-defined integrity.

We illustrate how the Integrity Analyzer could be used to obtain a rating of adherence to entity integrity. The entity integrity function checks that all primary and candidate keys for each table are unique and non-null.

To check entity integrity, the Integrity Analyzer user selects Entity Integrity from the data integrity pull-down menu and selects the Define tab. In the Define list box the user selects the fields that are primary and candidate keys for each table. Next, the user selects the Measure tab and asks the system to measure the number of violations of entity integrity. After the assessment has been completed, the user can select the Analyze tab and have the violation statistics displayed in numerical, graphical, or report form. Selecting the Improve tab produces a data object that displays the violation instances. The Referential integrity check works in a similar manner.

Screens corresponding to the functions of defining, measuring, analyzing, and improving entity integrity are shown in figure 4.1.

Similar procedures would be followed to perform referential and column integrity checks. To perform checks based on specific business rules, the user-defined integrity feature would be used.

Having chosen the user-defined integrity function, the user is presented with a display of conditions that have been defined. The user can now edit an existing condition or add a new user-defined rule. If the user selects Add, the system displays a Define window that elicits the information necessary to define a condition.

As in the previous examples, selection of the Measurement function evaluates the database for violation of this rule. Selection of the Analysis function displays the results of the assessment. Selection of the Improvement function results in a display of the records that violate the condition.

The user-defined constraints, however, are application-dependent. They vary from application to application and from industry to industry. Furthermore, these application-dependent constraints evolve over time. The Integrity Analyzer can be customized for a specific company within a specific industry by coding these user-defined rules in the software.

The Integrity Analyzer is more than simply an implementation of Codd's integrity constraints in relational database software. Unlike the standard commercial relational database management systems (RDBMS) packages that check for adherence to Codd's constraints when data are entered into the database, the Integrity Analyzer is a diagnostic tool that can assess the degree to which existing databases adhere to all the constraints defined by Codd as well as application-dependent user-defined rules. As a diagnostic tool, it delivers an analysis of the data repository's current quality state and suggests where improvements can be made.

Clearly, software to perform the preceding functions can be developed in-house as part of the database function. The purpose of the example was to illustrate how some of the metrics can be assessed and analyzed in an automated fashion. How each organization chooses to implement the subjective and quantitative measurements remains a decision within the organization.

Here we have focused on the measures that can be used to assess specific variables or dimensions of data quality. The amount of data that must be assessed can be quite voluminous, however. In chapter 5 we present an overview of principles and techniques that can be applied to assessing a large database repository using sampling techniques.

Process-Embedded Data Integrity Approach

In chapter 3 we briefly introduced the process-embedded data integrity approach. Here we elaborate on this technique by illustrating how a

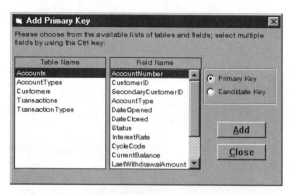

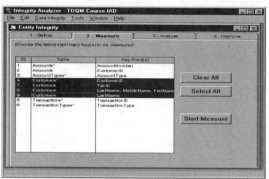

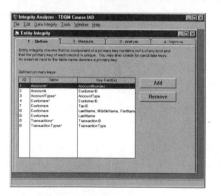

Figure 4.1
Entity Integrity Implementation
Source: Cambridge Research Group (CRG 1997b).

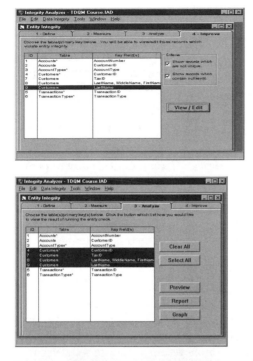

Figure 4.1 (continued)

global manufacturer of consumer goods, Glocom, made use of it. The example is excerpted from the larger action research study that appeared in Lee et al. (2004).

Glocom, a consumer goods manufacturing company with subsidiaries in 52 countries, produces health, cleansing, and household products. Its corporate culture is friendly, international, and nonconfrontational. Glocom's information technology infrastructure is advanced; it typically adopts new information practices and technology early. It has up-to-date database systems and has been experimenting with data quality improvement projects for several years.

Glocom's first iterations of the TDQM cycle focused on column integrity. The automated tool that Glocom embedded in the process was the Integrity Analyzer. Integrity violations were expected because the column integrity rules had not been consistently applied in the legacy systems. Table 4.1 summarizes the results from Glocom's many column integrity cycles in terms of the following five activities:

• *Identifying the problem.*   The column integrity rule for cases booked, non-negative values, was tested using the Integrity Analyzer software to measure violations, producing the sample results in figure 4.2. Negative values were discovered in the CASE_BK (cases booked) field.

• *Diagnosing the problem.*   The analyst examining these violations took them to the data quality manager for interpretation. From experience, the data quality manager surmised a possible legitimate meaning for the negative values: cancellations. He confirmed this interpretation with sales managers.

• *Planning the solution.*   Using this diagnosis, the analyst and managers searched for a solution that would capture cancellations but not interfere with the standard interpretation of cases booked. They decided to create a new field for cancellations and remove these data from the "cases booked" field.

• *Implementing the solution.*   This change was reflected at all relevant data levels—the operational database as well as the data warehouse.

• *Reflecting and learning.*   Using an explicit iterative process for column integrity improvement facilitated communications between the data quality manager and the sales managers, which facilitated further column integrity improvement cycles. The data quality manager also learned to use the process-embedded data integrity tool to add new constraints and modify constraints as new requirements developed. For example, to detect new values created by sales, he programmed additional

Table 4.1
A Process-Embedded Column Integrity Example

Identifying the problem	For shipment data, CASE_BK column, acceptable values should not be negative. (*Define*) Check shipment data, CASE_BK column, for values that are less than zero. (*Measure*)
Diagnosing the problem	Review of violation records shows negative values for number of cases booked. (*Analyze*) Data quality manager communicates with sales managers to determine the validity of negative bookings. (*Analyze*)
Planning the solution	Sales managers confirm that negative values represent canceled bookings. (*Analyze*) Data quality manager and sales managers jointly decide, "This is confusing." (*Analyze*) Data quality manager with approval from sales managers decides to add new field for canceled bookings. (*Analyze*)
Implementing the solution	New field for canceled bookings, CASE_CNL, is added to the shipment data. (*Improve*) Canceled bookings are removed from CASE_BK column and added to the new field. (*Improve*)
Reflecting and learning	Data quality manager learned to use the process-embedded data integrity tool to support problem solving. Sales managers learned to understand processes for exceptional cases and to communicate explicitly with data quality manager. Use of explicit iterative process for column integrity improvement facilitated communications between data quality manager and sales managers.

CASE_BK	DOL_BK	AST_CUST_ID	PROD_ID	WK_ID
-17	0	69000	90095	199841
-7	0	69000	90096	199841
-6	0	155450	1943	199738
-1	0	348000	90097	199643
-12	0	465600	90095	199633
-49	0	541800	90095	199710

Figure 4.2
Sample Column Integrity Results

user-defined rules into the tool. Over time the sales managers learned the processes for exceptional cases and communicated directly with the data quality manager.

This example illustrates a common problem in legacy data over time: fields are used for purposes other than originally intended. The dynamic nature of data drives this behavior. In this example column integrity for the cases booked remained as initially defined, and a new field was added to represent canceled bookings. In other cases the column integrity definition may be adjusted to fit the revised field use. With automatically enforced integrity in relational databases, if a salesperson needs to enter data not within range, such as negative bookings, he should follow a standard procedure of requesting a database change. Organizations should be aware, however, that integrity constraints can be misused in relational database management systems, for example, by recording "cancellation" in a comment field and using a positive value. Thus, regular monitoring of column integrity is still necessary.

Concluding Remarks

In this chapter we suggested some canonical forms that quantitative metrics can take on, and presented instantiations of these forms for a sample group of data quality dimensions.

Having well-defined metrics, however, does not eliminate the need to perform the actual measurements. One would prefer to have an automated system to measure these dimensions. To make the necessary measurements manually on a relatively large database can be an onerous task. To illustrate one approach to automating the process of large-scale measurement, we presented a prototype package, the Integrity Analyzer, which has been used by a number of organizations in their assessment of data quality. We further illustrated the technique of embedding data integrity software, specifically the Integrity Analyzer, in the TDQM process.

If one is dealing with a large-scale measurement task with a very large database, it may not be feasible to examine every unit of data, and accepted sampling techniques must be applied. Chapter 5 discusses auditing the data.

5

Sampling for Data Quality Assurance

It is not always feasible to perform a census of the database or data warehouse to obtain values for the required metrics. Taking a census, that is, examining all the records, may be too expensive and time-consuming. Indeed, for production databases and large data warehouses, millions of rows in a table are typical. Under these circumstances, the analyst must resort to traditional sampling methods that will meet the level of risk (sampling error) and precision desired or deemed acceptable.

In this chapter we first review concepts of sampling and a number of basic sampling methods. We discuss the use of a number of these methods in auditing a database or data warehouse for quality. We then present how these methods can be implemented in practice in a relational database management systems (RDBMS) environment, namely, through structured query language (SQL) queries.

Fundamental Concepts

We begin by briefly reviewing the basic concepts of sampling and relating them to the specific context, auditing a database or data warehouse. More detailed information and advanced techniques can be obtained from any classic textbook on sampling theory (Cochran 1977; Yamane 1967) and auditing (Guy, Carmichael, and Whittington 1998).

Statisticians identify two types of sampling methods: probability sampling and nonprobability sampling. In probability sampling, each unit is drawn from the population with known probability. In nonprobability sampling, one cannot state what is the probability of drawing a specific unit from the population. Thus, although the sample drawn may be representative of the population, there is no way of evaluating the reliability of the results. The probability method is the one used in most studies and is the method underlying the techniques discussed in this chapter.

When undertaking sampling, a number of items of importance must be addressed.

The first task is to set the objective of the sampling. In the present context the objective typically will be to determine error rates among the records in a table of the database. The ultimate goal is to obtain a good estimate of the population parameter of interest. For most of the metrics of interest, the population parameter to be estimated is a proportion. This can be either the percentage of errors or the percentage of nonerrors.

A second important task is to clearly identify the elementary or basic unit and the population, which consists of all the elementary units. In the context of auditing databases, the most common elementary unit is the record, and the population is all the records of a table. Note that even though one may be sampling to assess the state of a particular field in the record, the elementary unit is still the record. In formal statistical parlance, the particular field would be referred to as the variable associated with the basic unit. Its value can vary from basic unit to basic unit.

For completeness we introduce the concepts of the sampling unit and the frame. It may well be that the elementary unit and sampling unit are the same. On the other hand, it is possible that they are not. In the latter case the actual items sampled are the sampling unit. In the database and data warehouse context, for all but the rarest of cases the row of a table is both the elementary unit and sampling unit. The frame is the body of data from which the sample is drawn. The frame represents the population. In the database environment the frame consists of all the records in a specific table and is identical to the population. In the more general case it is possible that the frame is not identical to the actual population but is a good representation of the population.

The analyst should also specify the degree of precision and the reliability level required. This specification indicates the amount of error at a specific reliability level that one can accept over repeated sampling experiments. This value directly affects the size of the sample chosen. There will always be a trade-off between precision, reliability, and sample size. Clearly, the larger the sample size, the greater the precision.

Finally, a method of measurement must be specified. Here *method* refers to the type of instrument used to perform the sampling. It does not refer to the sampling design, that is, how the sampling will be accomplished. In the database environment we use direct measurement (observation) of the specific data element. Note that in the case of the Information Quality Assessment (IQA) survey described in chapter 3, if sampling of individual stakeholders were used, the method of measurement would be the survey instrument.

A simple example will help to illustrate these basic concepts. Assume we have a CUSTOMER table in our database. Our goal is to estimate the percentage of records in which the street address has been left blank. In this case we are interested in estimating a proportion, the ratio of blanks to total number of records. The elementary unit in this case is the record (row) of the CUSTOMER table. The population is the set of all records (rows) in the CUSTOMER table. In this example the sampling unit is also a record (row) of the CUSTOMER table, and the frame is the complete CUSTOMER table. The method is direct observation of data. We might require that the precision of the sample estimate be within .05 of the actual population proportion at a reliability of 95 percent.

If, for example, we were interested in knowing the percentage of primary key field values that were null in the database, then although the elementary unit would still be a row, the sampling unit and the frame might be different. Suppose we had a very large database and could not sample every table in the database. If a subset of tables were chosen from which the elementary units would be drawn, the sample unit would then be a table, and the frame would be the totality of elements contained in the tables selected.

The ultimate goal is to obtain a good estimate of the population parameter of interest. In order to reach this goal, a valid sampling procedure and an appropriate sample size must be chosen.

Selecting a Sampling Procedure

A number of sampling procedures are available to the data quality analyst. Which one is selected will be dictated by the problem and the constraints imposed by the environment. The typical approach is to first decide which sampling procedure is appropriate. Then the estimators of the parameters of interest, such as the proportion of defectives, are specified. The precision at a certain level of reliability must be specified. This will be used to determine the sample size needed.

Although many variations exist, the data quality analyst can choose from one of four main categories of sampling procedures.

Simple Random Sample

Using a random number generator, one draws a random sample of the size required. Thus if the table being sampled contains N rows, and the sample size is n, we generate a series of n random numbers whose values fall between 1 and N. These will be the rows used to obtain the estimate.

Systematic Sample

A variation on the simple random sample is systematic sampling. Again assuming that we are sampling the rows of a specific table, the first row to be examined is randomly chosen. Once the starting row is identified, every kth row from then on is included in the sample (k is the ratio of the table size to the sample size). In practice, the systematic sample approach makes the process of picking a sample a little easier than using pure random sampling.

Stratified Random Sample

If one believes that the quality of the data is not uniform, that is, if a certain subset of the data is more likely to have errors than another subset, one might want to ensure that those parts of the table are adequately represented in the sample. One could do this by creating subgroups (strata) such that the quality of data within each stratum is relatively uniform, and take simple random samples from each stratum. For example, if the data in each row of a table is arranged in ascending sequence of key field value, and we have additional knowledge that the key field values in the higher rows of the table are more prone to have errors than the beginning rows of the table, we could use this approach. The table could be divided into two halves, each defined as a stratum. Random samples could then be chosen from each of the strata or subsets.

Cluster Sample

In cluster sampling, the population is divided into clusters based on specific criteria. A subset of clusters is chosen at random. Either all the elementary units in a cluster are examined, or a random sample from each chosen cluster is inspected. This could be useful when one is combining different tables into a data warehouse. Such a scheme might be applicable when migrating data from different databases to a data warehouse under conditions that do not allow examination of all the tables in all the databases. Each table could be considered a cluster. A subset of tables could then be selected randomly. All rows in the table, or a random sample of the rows in the table, could be examined.

Of the four schemes, the one that is applied most frequently is the standard random sample.

Determining the Sample Size

The issue of sample size is an important one. Although resource constraints play an important role, the major consideration is the amount of error that the user is willing to tolerate. Many of the metrics relating to data quality are proportions. The formula for deciding on the size of the sample when estimating a proportion is $n = z^2 p(1 - p)/e^2$, where n is the sample size chosen, p is a preliminary estimate of the proportion, z is the two-tailed value of a standardized normal distribution, and e is the desired precision or acceptable error. Estimating p can be a challenge. Since the largest sample size will result when p is set to .5, in the absence of any information about p, the value of .5 can be used. If, however, the analyst can justify assuming another value of p, that value should be used. Often, a preliminary sample is taken to estimate the value of p. As long as the true proportion of defective rows is between 30 percent and 70 percent, the formula will serve well. One would hope that this is not the prevalent state of most databases.

A simple example illustrates the procedure. Assume that the goal is to estimate the proportion of customer records with null street addresses. Further assume that we will accept an error value of .01 at a reliability or confidence level of 95 percent ($z = 1.96$). To be conservative we estimate the true proportion to be .5. For these conditions, the sample size n

would be $n = (1.96)^2(.5)(.5)/(.01)^2 = 9,604$. Thus, if the table had 1 million rows, we would need to sample only about 1 percent of the rows in the table.

If the number of defective records is very low, alternative ways to determine the sample size will have to be used. Rare occurrences require a sample size of sufficient magnitude to ensure that a good estimate is achieved. One method is to predetermine the number of defective records (m) to be found in the sample and to continue sampling record by record until that number has been achieved. Although this method permits calculation of the true proportion of defective records, it is not a very practical method because the sample size is a random variable.

A rule of thumb suggests setting the expected number of defective records in the sample to be at least 2 (Gitlow et al. 1989). The minimum sample size required should satisfy the inequality $n \geq 2.00/(1 - \Pi)$, where Π represents the true proportion of acceptable rows. (Π can be estimated based on anecdotal evidence.) Clearly, a larger sample will yield a more precise estimate and hence a higher degree of confidence in the estimate.

The following example illustrates the application of this rule. Assume that z is 1.96 and e is .01, as in the preceding example. Prior knowledge of Π, however, indicates that it should be about .999 (0.1 percent nulls). Using the rule of thumb, the minimum sample size required is 2,000. If we had applied the standard formula, we would have obtained a sample size of 39, which would be much too small.

Performing Sampling in a Transaction Database Environment

Any of the objective metrics presented in chapter 4 may require estimation. Having a good sampling design and the appropriate sample size does not remove the challenge of carrying out the actual sampling. Performing this task can be helped by a feature provided by modern relational database management systems, specifically, the SQL query language. SQL queries, which are relatively easy to construct, can be used to implement the sampling procedures chosen. To some extent, software that automates the assessment process, such as the Integrity Analyzer described in chapter 4, also can aid in implementing a sampling program.

A number of operators, functions, and limiting clauses of SQL are quite helpful in obtaining values that can be used in the metrics we have previously discussed. For example, the COUNT function can be used to obtain a tally of the number of rows that contain a specific value or meet a given condition. To illustrate, suppose a CUSTOMER table consists of four columns: CUSTOMER_ID, CUSTOMER_NAME, CUSTOMER_ADDRESS, CUSTOMER_BALANCE. For the sake of simplicity, assume that the complete address is in one column. Now we can obtain a count of the number of rows with the SQL statement

```
SELECT COUNT(CUSTOMER_ID)
  FROM CUSTOMER;
```

If we wish to obtain a tally of rows where the CUSTOMER_ID is null, then we can use the statement

```
SELECT COUNT(CUSTOMER_ID)
  FROM CUSTOMER
    WHERE CUSTOMER_ID IS NULL;
```

If we wish to obtain a tally of the rows whose balance is between $0 and $1 million, we could write

```
SELECT COUNT(CUSTOMER_ID)
  FROM CUSTOMER
    WHERE CUSTOMER_BALANCE BETWEEN 0 AND 1000000;
```

Alternatively, if we wanted a tally of those rows whose balances are outside these limits, we could write

```
SELECT COUNT(CUSTOMER_ID)
  FROM CUSTOMER
    WHERE CUSTOMER_BALANCE < 0 OR CUSTOMER_BALANCE >
    1000000;
```

These examples illustrate the relative ease of use of SQL to obtain tallies. They assume that all the rows in the CUSTOMER table are being examined, that a census is being taken. The focus of this chapter, however, is the case where one cannot take a census and must sample. Here again SQL proves useful. The language allows one to generate random integers (corresponding to rows in a table) to select a subset of rows to make up a sample. Different dialects of SQL vary in how the statement to generate a random number is constructed. For example, in Microsoft's SQL, the number generation function is RND. Regardless of the exact expression, the different dialects allow for the random selection of rows in a table. Thus a sample of rows from the complete table can be obtained.

Having the ability to generate a randomly chosen subset of rows and to perform tallies while imposing different conditions allows one to obtain values for many of the metrics discussed in chapter 4. In what follows, we discuss the application of these techniques to assessing adherence to Codd's integrity constraints. As we pointed out, these rules represent a small subset of the basic data quality dimensions. They do serve particularly well, however, as examples of practical applications of the techniques presented in this chapter.

Many would argue that the tests we are about to describe are superfluous because the imposition of entity integrity constraints by the database management system would never allow violations of entity integrity to occur in the database. Unfortunately, costly experience shows that corruption of the database does occur and that violations may exist and deserve to be addressed.

Entity Integrity

Two potential violations of entity integrity can occur: either the value of the key field is null, or the value of the key field is not unique.

Examining the case in which the value of the key field is null, the objective is to determine what percentage of the population has null keys. This reduces to estimating a proportion. Any appropriate technique to estimate proportions could be applied here. It would appear that simple random sampling would be a usable technique to apply.

The second case (nonuniqueness) presents a more formidable challenge. Ideally, one would take a row and compare it to all other rows and decide if duplication of key field value exists. One might do this for each row, keeping track of which duplicates have already been tallied. This is not feasible for most large relational databases. Knowing the number of rows in the table, one could use SQL to count the distinct values. For example, the SQL statement for the CUSTOMER table would be

```
SELECT COUNT (DISTINCT CUSTOMER_ID)
   FROM CUSTOMER;
```

The difference between the total number of rows and the tally of distinct values of CUSTOMER_ID would give a measure of the number of duplicates. Even this might not be feasible. Then one could resort to random sampling. Specifying required values for the formulas to compute sample size, one could compute the required sample size. One could then apply SQL statements to select the random sample and assess the number of violations.

Column Integrity

The column integrity constraint requires that the values in a column are drawn from a set of permissible values. The violations of column integrity can take on a number of forms:

- Blank value
- Null value
- Nonunique values (if so mandated for a column that does not represent a primary key)
- Value not in a valid set of numeric discrete values or alphanumeric values
- Value not in a valid numeric range (continuous)

The checks for blank values, null values, and nonunique values can be done using the same methods that were suggested for entity integrity checks and illustrated in the applications of SQL. For checking values simple random sampling would be appropriate. There is the possibility, however, that the distribution of these discrete values is not uniform across the records. In that case a stratified sampling approach might be appropriate. The sampling method chosen would depend on the characteristics of the records with respect to values in the specific column of interest. Checking that values come from a list of valid characters would be handled in the same fashion as checking for numeric values from a discrete list of numeric values.

If we are interested in simply determining whether a value is within a range, we are faced with estimating a percentage (binomial). This would be addressed in the same fashion as the previous situations of estimating a binomial parameter. Once the sample has been generated, the rows can be assessed using the SQL statement with the BETWEEN operator.

Referential Integrity

The violation of referential integrity poses an interesting challenge. A violation occurs when the value of a foreign key in one table does not match an existing primary key in the associated table. If the foreign key field value is null, however, then there is no violation of referential integrity. In a very large relation how does one know which foreign keys are null? Here is a case where SQL provides a quick answer. A simple SQL query like

```
SELECT *
  FROM [name of table]
    WHERE [name of foreign key] NOT NULL;
```

will yield the records whose foreign field value is not null and that will form the population from which the sample will be drawn. The SQL capability of INSERT INTO allows for the generation of a table from which all null foreign keys have been eliminated. An appropriate random sample can now be generated from this new table.

A second challenge remains: how should one handle the matching? One can randomly select a sample from the foreign keys. This requires that each of the primary key field values be checked until a match is found. Although it is possible that checking the primary table for a match may be computationally prohibitive, primary tables usually have many fewer entries than the dependent tables whose foreign keys provide the linkage to the primary table. For example, a table may have 20 rows, each representing a different department. The employee table, which contains the employees in those 20 departments, may have 100 or 1,000 rows. Thus the check for matches may not be overwhelming.

An alternative approach would be to perform an SQL outer join. One could then construct the appropriate SQL query to select those rows where the primary and foreign key fields (columns) do not match, that is, those rows in which one of the two is null. The resulting table should have a small number of rows and could then be examined in total. We would not expect large numbers of referential integrity violations. Nevertheless, if this were the case, the large numbers of violations would be discerned on construction of the table with the SQL query.

Expanding the Environment: Distributed Databases and Data Warehouses

Assessment of data quality is not limited to evaluating traditional centralized transaction databases. Creating data warehouses and data marts, and the software support to manipulate these, is a standard undertaking for most large firms. These data warehouses, however, must be assessed for data quality. A prevailing view assumes that the data entering a data warehouse has been cleansed and is of high quality, but this view is not consistent with reality. At best, the cleansed data has been checked for factual correctness or for completeness but would not be considered data of high quality from the multidimensional perspective we have espoused. Indeed, such errors as inconsistencies in data type for the same field appearing in different parts of the data warehouse occur often. One cannot assume that the data warehouse has data of good quality, and as a consequence some sampling of the data must be undertaken.

Earlier we mentioned that a cluster sample design might be appropriate when migrating data to a data warehouse. The base tables would be audited for data quality within this sampling design. Once the data warehouse has been created, the techniques discussed in conjunction with a transaction database could be applied.

Apart from data warehouses, databases are increasingly being distributed. This poses the challenge of how and what to sample when the database is distributed. If the approach is to have a central database and local replication of parts of the data, the sampling approach differs from the one where the database is distributed with minimal redundancy and no central site.

The case of a multiple-site processing, multiple-site data-distributed environment serves as an interesting example. Here we would have a set of heterogeneous distributed databases. More than likely, some sort of stratified sampling would take place at the individual database level. This would be reasonable if there were prior knowledge that some of the databases are of higher (or lower) data quality than others. Alternatively, the analyst might randomly choose a subset of databases to sample. In any event, once the basic sampling design has been constructed, the techniques discussed in connection with the single database table case apply.

Concluding Remarks

In this chapter we discussed some of the basic concepts and techniques that can be used to audit a relational database. The discussion focused on some basic concepts of sampling and some basic SQL constructs. In combination, these provide a powerful tool for the data quality analyst. The sampling constructs are applicable to the assessment of individual perceptions of data quality discussed in chapter 3 and to the assessment of the quantitative metrics presented in chapter 4. The SQL constructs are relevant to performing measurements for the quantitative metrics. With these tools in hand, the analyst can begin obtaining the measurements that contribute substantively to the awareness of data quality and that form the basis for the diagnostic approach advocated in earlier chapters.

In the forthcoming chapters we examine the issues that must be addressed once data quality awareness has been achieved and baseline data quality assessments have been completed.

6

Understanding the Anatomy of Data Quality Problems and Patterns

In chapters 2–5 we presented methods, tools, and techniques that organizations can use to assess and audit the status of data quality. Understanding the status of an organization's current data quality readiness sets the stage for improving data quality. Improving data quality, however, cannot be achieved without fully understanding the highly complex nature and the magnitude of data quality issues in the comprehensive context, including the organizational context. For example, a data consumer states, "I cannot access this data." This statement might indicate a relatively complex situation that involves the interaction of several data quality aspects such as security issues, the inability to find the information, or a misunderstanding as to how the information is named or represented. In addition, a data quality survey might also confirm a perception of very low accessibility within the organization. Typically, this seemingly simple data quality problem does not occur in isolation. It involves accumulated, lengthy, and hidden processes, and signals root conditions leading to data consumers' experience of difficulties with using data. To effectively improve data quality, therefore, organizations must carefully diagnose and improve not only the data but also the data environment in the specific context. By data environment we mean the areas related to collecting, storing, and using data. The data environment includes not only database systems and information systems infrastructure but also related task process mechanisms, rules, methods, actions, policies, and culture that together typify and impact an organization's data quality. Data quality problems do not exist only in the automated computer environment. Problems can arise in manual business processes or in the combination of manual and computerized environments. The patterns and solutions discussed here can be used in both manual and automated environments.

In this chapter we identify and analyze ten root conditions that can develop into data quality problems in an organization. We then suggest intervention actions that organizations can take to prevent or redirect the negative progression of the root conditions and improve data quality. This chapter extends the seminal work by Strong, Lee, and Wang (1997a; 1997b) and makes use of the material in those sources.

Ten Root Conditions of Data Quality Problems

The ten root conditions presented here were distilled from detailed embedded case studies and content analysis of data quality projects in leading organizations. These are common root conditions, which over time can lead to data quality problems if not addressed. Alternatively, these conditions present opportunities for data quality improvement if appropriate intervention is initiated. Interventions can be either temporary short-term patches or longer-term solutions. Clearly, the longer-term solutions are the more appropriate and desirable interventions.

The ten root conditions are as follows:

1. *Multiple data sources.* Multiple sources of the same information produce different values for this information. This can include values that were accurate at a given point in time.

2. *Subjective judgment in data production.* Information production using subjective judgment can result in the production of biased information.

3. *Limited computing resources.* Lack of sufficient computing resources limits accessibility to relevant information.

4. *Security/accessibility trade-off.* Easy access to information may conflict with requirements for security, privacy, and confidentiality.

5. *Coded data across disciplines.* Coded data from different functions and disciplines is difficult to decipher and understand. Also, codes may conflict.

6. *Complex data representations.* Algorithms are not available for automated content analysis across instances of text and image information. Non-numeric information can be difficult to index in a way that permits location of relevant information.

7. *Volume of data.*   Large volumes of stored information make it difficult to access needed information in a reasonable time.

8. *Input rules too restrictive or bypassed.*   Input rules that are too restrictive may impose unnecessary controls on data input and lose data that has important meaning. Data entry clerks may skip entering data into a field (missing information) or arbitrarily change a value to conform to rules and pass an edit check (erroneous information).

9. *Changing data needs.*   As information consumers' tasks and the organization environment (such as new market, new legal requirements, new trends) change, the information that is relevant and useful changes.

10. *Distributed heterogeneous systems.*   Distributed heterogeneous systems without proper integration mechanisms lead to inconsistent definitions, formats, rules, and values. The original meaning of data may be lost or distorted as data flows and is retrieved from a different system, time, place, data consumer, for same or different purposes.

1. Multiple Data Sources

Multiple sources of the same information produce different values for this information. Database design recommendations warn against storing and updating the same data in multiple places because ensuring consistent updating of multiple copies is difficult. Similarly, using several different processes is likely to produce different values for the same information. For example, a hospital produces an illness severity assessment for intensive care unit (ICU) patients using two different procedures: (1) a specialist evaluates the patient at admission, and (2) an ICU nurse observes the patient during her stay. Not surprisingly, these two assessments can differ. Billing and other reporting contexts, however, require one consistent value.

Such situations arise frequently in organizations because systems designed for different purposes, such as clinical use and financial use, may require the same information as input, for example, illness severity. Autonomous development of these systems results in parallel but slightly different procedures for collecting the same information.

Typically, generating the same information from multiple sources causes serious problems. For instance, hospitals can experience financial and legal problems if billing information generates higher reimbursement than clinical information warrants. Or, consumers may stop using the information because inconsistencies lead them to question its believability.

This root condition is often overlooked. The multiple production procedures continue to operate and produce different information values. The condition may be hidden from information consumers because they use different systems—for instance, clinical consumers access clinical information, whereas others access financial information—or all consumers may gravitate to one source. Alternatively, information may be downloaded selectively to information consumers. For a short-term improvement intervention, an organization can keep both systems but use one for billing purposes. It can determine when there are process improvement opportunities if there are always differences in the illness severity assessment.

Moving beyond quick fixes requires the reexamining the information production processes. How should the information be produced? For example, one of the hospitals we studied decided on a common definition for ICU illness severity and a production process that would consistently define it. Its computer systems were changed to implement this process.

Long-term interventions would include instituting a rule that does not allow synonyms: different groups should not use different names for the same data item or procedure. In addition, a rule that prohibits homonyms should be instituted: data items representing different things should not have the same name. If for valid reasons homonyms are allowed, they should be documented in the data dictionary, and this knowledge should be shared across the organization.

2. Subjective Judgment in Data Production

Information production using subjective judgment produces biased information. Information stored in an organization's database is considered to be a set of facts. The process by which these "facts" are collected, however, may involve subjective judgment. The illness severity assessment mentioned previously is one example. Another example is medical codes assigned to indicate the disease diagnosed and the procedures performed on a patient. Despite rules for assigning codes, medical coders necessarily exercise judgment in selecting the appropriate codes.

Recognizing that subjective judgment was used in producing the information, information consumers may avoid using such information. Thus, information collected using costly human judgment procedures may not provide sufficient benefit to the organization to make it worth collecting.

Such data problems are often hidden from data consumers because the extent to which judgment is involved in creating it is unknown to them. They may believe that information stored in computer systems is more factual than is warranted. Patching the problem means adding more production rules to handle the variance in information produced from similar underlying facts.

We do not propose eliminating human judgment from information production. This would severely restrict the information available to consumers because some information can be produced only subjectively. Longer-term fixes would include better and extended training for data collectors, improvement of the data collectors' knowledge of the business domain, and clear statement and communication about how specific subjective judgments are to be made.

3. Limited Computing Resources

Lack of sufficient computing resources limits access to relevant information. For example, an airline company used unreliable communication lines with insufficient capacity to access and maintain spare parts inventory information for aircraft. As a result, not all inventory transactions were recorded, leading to inaccurate and incomplete information. A health maintenance organization (HMO) did not provide terminals to all employees, which reduced access to information and productivity. Furthermore, some tasks were accomplished without the complete information, which resulted in poor decision making.

Although most of today's knowledge workers have computers in their offices and have reliable communication lines, computing resources are still limited. For example, in today's increasingly wired environment, bandwidth becomes a limited resource. There will always be requests for newer, faster, better-equipped computers with higher bandwidth communication lines. As information consumers complain, this problem is solved in the short term by providing more computing power.

As a longer-term solution, some organizations have developed technology upgrade policies. For example, some universities have decided that computers in student labs should be upgraded periodically to meet the current computer system standard. In addition, funding for more computing resources may be allocated to consumers' budgets to ensure the

best use of funds by data consumers. More efficient use of existing computers is likely when data consumers are charged for computer use.

4. Security Accessibility Trade-off

Easy access to information may conflict with requirements for security, privacy, and confidentiality. For data consumers high-quality information must be easily accessible. Ensuring privacy, confidentiality, and security of information, however, requires barriers to access. Thus these accessibility and security goals for high-quality information are in conflict. For example, patients' medical records contain confidential information, yet analysts need access to these records for research studies and management decision making. Protecting patient privacy can be achieved, for example, by requiring legal department permissions to use patient records. For consumers the need to obtain advanced permission is a barrier to information access.

A short-term fix is to apply ad hoc solutions to privacy, confidentiality, or security problems as they arise. For example, if a patient's human immunodeficiency virus (HIV) status is released unintentionally, new procedures are developed to prevent a recurrence. These new procedures can be developed to minimize barriers to accessibility for legitimate tasks.

Moving beyond the short-term patches requires developing privacy, confidentiality, and security policies and procedures for all information when it is first collected. Based on these policies, consistent standard procedures need to be developed for assessing needs for access with minimal effort and time delays. Information consumers typically recognize the need for privacy, confidentiality, and security of information and are willing to abide by reasonable rules. This will hold, however, only if the new definitions and meanings of security and confidentiality are communicated and shared across the organization.

5. Coded Data across Disciplines

Coded data from different professional areas are difficult to decipher and understand. With technological advances, it is possible to collect and store many types of information, including text and images. Electronics storage itself is not the primary issue. Representing this information for easy entry and easy access is the important issue.

For example, consider notes on patient care in hospitals. Medical coders read these notes and summarize them into Disease-Related Group codes for billing (Fetter 1991), but the detailed notes remain in paper form because of the cost of converting them to electronic form. Deciphering the notes and typing them is time-consuming. Some information, especially the patient discharge summary, is dictated by the doctor and then transcribed into electronic form. More doctors are entering data electronically, and increasingly hospitals are using electronic forms. Advances in imaging technology make it easier to store and retrieve images.

With information technology storage and retrieval capabilities continually improving, organizations need to decide how much and what type of information to store. In the case of codes, the necessary business domain knowledge, such as medical and engineering, to fully interpret codes must be imparted to information consumers. To do so properly, the knowledge of the experts should be codified and made available. This will take place over the long term.

To the extent possible, different codes for the same classification should be mapped. It is preferable to settle on one code. When such a solution is not possible, it may be more cost-effective to maintain a map. A situation to avoid is incurring the high cost of storing this information electronically with little or no improvement in the quality of information delivered to information consumers.

6. Complex Data Representations

Currently, advanced algorithms are not available for automated content analysis across instances of text and image information. Such non-numeric information can be difficult to index in a way that permits location of relevant information.

Although information consumers can access non-numeric information and information distributed across multiple systems, they need more than access. They need to aggregate, manipulate, and identify trends. This problem is manifested as information that is technically available to information consumers but is difficult or impossible to analyze.

Analysts and medical researchers need to analyze electronic images in the same way they analyze quantitative information by using statistical summary and trend analysis techniques. For this reason, one of the hospitals we studied did not electronically store all text and images. Electronic storage of this information would not be sufficiently beneficial until the hospital can automate the analysis of several X-rays, for example, to determine whether a patient is developing pneumonia, and can compute trends across multiple X-rays to study the tendency of ICU patients to develop pneumonia.

Hospitals need to assess trends in patient treatments. The treatment information to do so is stored as notes from doctors and nurses. The medical industry partially handles this by using coding systems to summarize text. To fully resolve this problem, it needs to resolve a related problem, the difficulty of analyzing information stored in different systems. Simply providing consumers with access to each system and its information does not solve the problem of analyzing trends across information stored in multiple systems with inconsistent definitions, names, or formats. This problem is also related to root condition 10, distributed heterogeneous systems.

This problem can be patched in a number of ways. For example, various coding systems are essentially patches to assist with the analysis of textual information. Routines to match fields across different systems assist with analyzing information across these systems. Such patches create further problems. First, the patches are piecemeal solutions to small parts of the problem, such as matching routines that are tailored to specific fields. To solve the entire problem, several patches are needed. Second, these patches may be incomplete or cause other problems. Matching names across systems, using Soundex algorithms for example, will fail to find some correct matches. Coding systems for summarizing information in an analyzable way generate analysis problems if information consumers are required to interpret the codes.

Longer-term solutions to these problems involve advances in information technology and its applications. Data warehouses and common data dictionaries can provide solutions to part of the problems addressed here, such as analyzing structured information across systems. Much progress is being made in algorithms for analyzing image information. In general, the capability for storing new forms of information always develops before full capabilities for analyzing that information is completed.

7. Volume of Data

Large volumes of stored information make it difficult to access needed information in a reasonable time. As has been often stated, "more information" is not necessarily better than "less information." Large volumes of information present problems for those responsible for storing and maintaining the information and for those searching for useful information. Consider, for example, a telephone company, which generates thousands of billing transactions hourly. Customers expect each telephone company representative to have immediate access to their billing records to resolve billing questions. Or, an HMO example. It generates over 1 million patient activity records yearly. For any particular disease, analyses of disease trends and procedures performed over a several-year period may involve only a few thousand records, but these must be selected from millions. The hospital has tens of thousands of patients each year. These generate 12 gigabytes of operational information yearly. Multiple-year trend analysis becomes a problem for the HMO.

Information systems professionals have at their disposal standard techniques for storing large amounts of information and providing efficient access to it. One such technique is using codes to condense textual information. For example, hospital systems store patients' religion using a coding scheme, such as 1 for religion A, 2 for religion B, and so on. Although such coding schemes are common, they can place an undue burden on consumers, who are responsible for interpreting the coded information displayed on computer screens. One consumer said, "I judge the quality of a computer system by the number of Post-its attached to the terminal." The Post-its are memory aids to consumers for interpreting what the displayed information actually means. This problem is also related to the root condition 5, coded data across disciplines. Newer and more advanced graphical user interfaces should help reduce such problems.

Longer-term fixes demand that requirements be gathered precisely and that analysis of the trade-off among the additional storage needed, additional query time incurred, and decision-making speed be performed. Clearly, data must be organized for easy retrieval and use. One way of improving accessibility is to provide aggregated information. Accomplishing this, however, is linked to obtaining an accurate representation of the information consumers' requirements.

In the HMO case the short-term solution was to perform a weekend batch extract, downloading the relevant records for historical analyses. This ad hoc download significantly increased the time required to access and analyze this information. The longer-term fix was to create an additional database containing a subset of the yearly operational information for the last dozen years. This new database, stored on an easy-to-access client/server system, was updated weekly. In designing and managing this database, the organization moved beyond patching to create a permanent solution for its large volume of information.

8.   Input Rules Too Restrictive or Bypassed

Too strict database editing rules that impose unnecessary controls on data input may cause data with important meaning to be lost. Input rules that are too restrictive may produce missing or erroneous information if data entry clerks strive to observe them by arbitrarily changing a value to fit into a field so as to pass an edit check, or are unable to fit a value into a field and so skip doing it.

As we have pointed out, improving data quality requires attention to more than just the dimension of accuracy. Such concerns as capturing the usability and usefulness of information must be considered. Thus our focus is not solely on errors but also on systemic and structured problems. Some errors in producing information are systemic problems, for example, the routine nonentry of information into computers. Although errors can occur anywhere in the information production processes, systemic errors occurring during production are especially important because they can be hidden from casual review and affect the entire system.

In the hospital case all codes for outpatient surgery performed were not entered into the HMO's computers because edit checks rejected these codes. This was discovered only when an analysis using this information produced suspicious results. An investigation revealed the routine nonentry of data. This had been occurring since the purchase of a new data entry system. Since the data entry clerks did not receive complaints, they assumed the information was not important. This information is now lost because it would be too costly and perhaps impossible to recover.

This condition is caused by hidden problems in the information production processes. A short-term solution would fix these problems as they are discovered. For example, the HMO used a temporary work-around of entering this information into a comment field until the next vendor software release. Moving beyond patching requires understanding, documenting, and controlling information processes in a similar way to how physical manufacturing processes are managed. Organizations should ensure that data collectors and data custodians understand the effects of good and bad data. In short, they must make data collection a part of the business process.

9. Changing Data Needs

As information consumers' tasks and the organization environment change, the information that is relevant and useful changes. Information is only of high quality if it meets the needs of data consumers. Providing the information that information consumers need is a difficult problem because there are multiple consumers, each with different needs. Furthermore, these needs change over time. Although an initial solution to consumers' information needs may be satisfactory, over time the quality of the solution will deteriorate.

In the hospital case reimbursement to hospitals changed from collecting fees based on the cost of individual procedures performed to collecting fixed fees by the disease of the patient as defined by Disease-Related Group codes. This necessitated processes for collecting and using information for billing that differed from those used to meet management information needs for analyzing costs.

This condition represents mismatches between the information provided to and the information needed by data consumers. When the problem becomes severe enough, it is patched by changing processes and computer systems. As mismatches develop, however, consumers develop various manual and computerized work-arounds to accomplish their tasks. Such work-arounds can become routine, and thus many small problems never grow severe enough to draw sufficient attention.

Moving to longer-term solutions requires planning for changes to information processes and systems, and anticipating changing information consumer needs before they become serious problems. This requires the continual review of the environment in which the business operates. Responsibility should be assigned for proactively managing data and matching data to future needs. Procedures should also be designed for flexibility in reporting. For example, the hospital anticipated the change in reimbursement procedures and changed its processes and systems before the change was implemented. Organizations that fail to act proactively will suffer severe financial problems.

10.   Distributed Heterogeneous Systems

Distributed heterogeneous systems without a proper integration mechanism lead to inconsistent definitions, formats, and values. With distributed heterogeneous systems, information can be accessed and analyzed as if it were in one location. Distributed systems add to an organization's capacities for storing information. Nevertheless, distributed systems exhibit unique problems, for example, inaccessibility of relevant information because of excessive time needed to select and aggregate the data.

The most common problem associated with distributed systems is inconsistent information, that is, information with different values or representations across systems. Information with different values may be generated from multiple sources or created by inconsistent updating of multiple copies. Information with different representations becomes a problem when integrating across autonomously designed systems. In the HMO example some divisions stored Disease-Related Group codes with decimal points and others without them. This required attention every time this information was integrated across divisions. Routines to handle such problems, whether manual or computerized, represent short-term patches.

Data warehouses are a popular current solution to distributed system problems. Rather than rewriting old, autonomously developed systems, a data warehouse is populated using extract routines that pull information from old systems and resolve inconsistencies. This presents a centralized, consistent front-end approach to distributed back-end systems. Note that developing a data warehouse or a data mart does not guarantee data quality without close collaboration among data collectors, data custodians, and data consumers. With this solution, front-end accessibility problems are reduced. Going beyond this, the organization should ensure that consistent procedures are instituted. Standards should be developed, where appropriate, that meet global needs and allow for local variations to the extent possible.

Manifestation of Data Quality Problems

The root conditions can evolve into manifestations that are either positive or negative. Figure 6.1 summarizes the evolution of these root conditions and shows the individual paths, in both directions, of the evolution. Tables 6.1 and 6.2 list warning signs, possible problems, and the results of short-term and long-term interventions. In this section we focus on those paths that lead to problem states. Although a root condition with early intervention can evolve to a positive state, we focus on the negative states because these are of greater interest from the perspective of circumventing the problem early on. As a root condition evolves into one of the general problems presented in figure 6.1, poor performance is detected along one or more of the traditional data quality dimensions. The techniques introduced in chapters 3, 4, and 5 can help in detecting this poor performance and in isolating the path and diagnosing the basic problem.

At the operational level, the root conditions manifest themselves in many ways. Among the most noticeable are that the data are not accessible, the data are difficult to use, or the data are not used at all. We examine the general problem category into which the root conditions can evolve and relate them to data quality dimensions.

Data Are Not Used

Mismatches among multiple sources of the same data are a common cause of data quality concerns. Initially, data consumers do not know the source to which quality problems should be attributed; they know only that the data are conflicting. Thus these concerns initially appear as *believability* problems. (To highlight the interaction of the data quality dimensions in a data quality project and to emphasize those dimensions that are pertinent to the development of a particular problem pattern (see figure 6.1), we italicize dimensions here.

Over time, information about the causes of mismatches accumulates from evaluations of the *accuracy* of different sources, which leads to a poor *reputation* for less accurate sources. A reputation for poor quality can also develop with little factual basis. As a reputation for poor-quality data becomes common knowledge, these data sources are viewed as having little *added value* for the organization, resulting in reduced use.

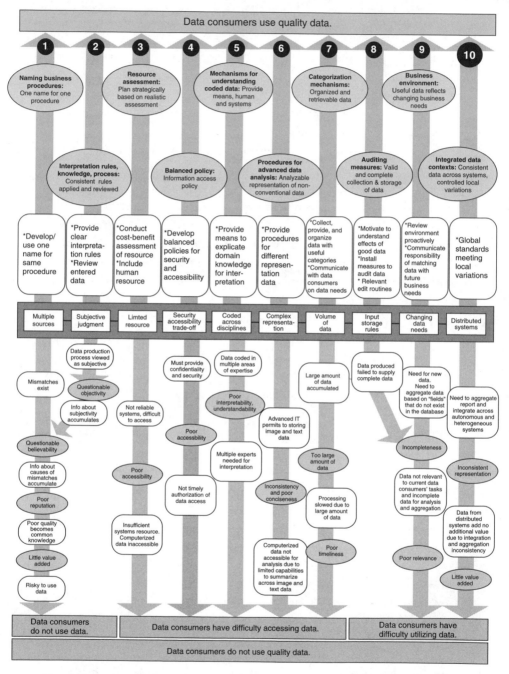

Figure 6.1
Manifestations of the Ten Root Conditions of Data Quality: Positive and Negative Paths

Subjective judgment in the data production process is another common cause. For example, coded or interpreted data are considered to be of lower quality than raw data. Initially, only those with knowledge of data production processes are aware of these potential problems. These appear as concerns about data *objectivity*. Over time, information about the subjective nature of data production accumulates, resulting in data of questionable *believability* and *reputation* and thus of little *added value* to data consumers. The overall result is reduced use of the suspect data.

Mismatches among multiple data sources are found in many organizations. For example, an airline company has a history of mismatches between its inventory system data and its physical warehouse counts. Warehouse counts serve as a standard against which to measure the *accuracy* of system data, that is, the system data source is inaccurate and not *believable* and is adjusted periodically to match actual warehouse counts. The system data gradually develops mismatches, however, and its *reputation* gradually worsens until the data is not used for decision making.

At a hospital mismatches occur between two databases. One database contains historical data (TRACE), and the other database contains operational short-term data (STATUS). The historical data in TRACE is extracted from the hospital's information and control system. It is used by managers to make long-term decisions and by medical researchers. The STATUS system records data that is a snapshot of daily hospital resources. Some data, such as, daily hospital bed utilization, are available from both systems. Nevertheless, they frequently have different values. Over time, TRACE develops a *reputation* as an *accurate* source, and the use of STATUS declines.

At an HMO inconsistent data values occur between internal HMO patient records and bills submitted by hospitals for reimbursement. For example, when the HMO is billed for coronary bypass surgery, the HMO patient record should indicate active, serious heart problems. Mismatches occur in both directions: hospital making claims at the same time that the HMO has no record of the problems, and HMO records indicating the existence of problems without the corresponding hospital claims. Initially, the HMO assumes that the external (hospital) data were wrong; the HMO perceives its data as being more *believable* and having a better

Table 6.1
Positive Manifestations of the Ten Root Conditions

Manifestations	Warning Signs	Impact of Problem
Condition 1—Multiple Data Sources		
Multiple sources of the same information produce different values for this information: the same piece of data is called by more than one name (synonym problem), or items that have the same name represent different things (homonym problem).	Different systems are developed for different purposes or for different parts of the organization that require the same information. The same information can be updated in more than one file.	Different values exist for the same fact. Information is inconsistent. Time is wasted reconciling differences. Financial and legal problems ensue. People think two data items are the same when they are not; they attempt to aggregate or classify the items as if they were the same, leading to erroneous and conflicting results.
Condition 2—Subjective Judgment in Data Production		
Information production using subjective judgment produces biased information.	Definite rules and constraints are not used to guide data input. Little or no edit checking is done for data input. Free-form text is used for data fields.	Unreliable and inaccurate data are entered and used.

Intervention Actions	Target State	Improved Data Use

Condition 1—Multiple Data Sources

Maintain only one source for the information. Allow updates of the information at only this source and replicate data from that source. Maintain a data dictionary or name repository to identify synonyms and homonyms. Document and communicate conflicting terms.	Data are updated or changed at only one source. Names and definitions for identical data are identical. Data contexts are mediated for special cases. No synonyms or homonyms exist.	Data with consistent names and definitions, which carry the original meaning of the data, are used by data consumers.

Condition 2—Subjective Judgment in Data Production

Business domain experts or data consumers review entered data. Provide better training for data collectors. Data entry clerks should have appropriate domain knowledge. Clearly state the interpretation rules for subjective judgments. Communicate that certain data are subjective.	Consistent interpretation of rules. Consistent edit checking. Maintenance of data repository with complete definitions.	Objective data are used by data consumers, or they are aware of the subjective nature of some data.

Table 6.1
(continued)

Manifestations	Warning Signs	Impact of Problem
Condition 3—Limited Computing Resources		
Lack of sufficient computing resources limits accessibility to relevant information: hardware or network resources are inadequate; coding schemes are arcane and not documented; multiple items are stored in one data field.	Data consumers complain about computing resources and their reliability. They cannot access or find needed information.	Lack of computing resources limits timely access to information. Inadequate documentation causes data to be hidden or lost.
Condition 4—Security/Accessibility Trade-off		
Ease of access to information conflicts with requirements for security, privacy, and confidentiality.	Privacy, security, and confidentiality are important, but data must be accessible to provide value.	Mechanisms for security are barriers to accessibility; data provide less value.
Condition 5—Coded Data across Disciplines		
Coded data from different functions and disciplines are difficult to decipher and understand. Codes may conflict.	Data from multiple specialties are used across organization.	Data are difficult to understand and not used in the proper context.

Intervention Actions	Target State	Improved Data Use
Condition 3—Limited Computing Resources		
Conduct cost/ benefit analysis. Establish realistic goals. Include human resources in resource assessment.	Realistic assessment of resources— infrastructure and competence.	Data in systems can be adequately accessed by data consumers.
Condition 4—Security/Accessibility Trade-off		
Develop consistent policies and procedures for security and accessibility. Need to share more information with all stakeholders: create a new definition of what security and confidentiality mean.	Balanced and consistent information access policy and use.	Data with accessibility and security are used appropriately by data consumers.
Condition 5—Coded Data across Disciplines		
Provide the means (expert systems, human) to achieve domain knowledge to fully interpret coded data. Map the different codes. When complete mapping is not possible, agree on a process to resolve mapping issues: usually adding new attributes to the object or record and new processes to maintain them.	All coded data are consistent and understandable. Code tables maintain understandable descriptions and meanings.	Understandable data are used by data consumers.

Table 6.1
(continued)

Manifestations	Warning Signs	Impact of Problem
Condition 6—Complex Data Representations		
Algorithms are not available for automated content analysis across instances of text and image information. Non-numeric information can be difficult to index in a way that permits location of relevant information.	Operational and managerial decisions require analysis across multiple image or text files.	Analysis of image and text data stored in electronic form is very limited.
Condition 7—Volume of Data		
With large volumes of stored data, it can be difficult to access needed information in a reasonable time.	Large amount of operational data with need for managerial or strategic analysis of this information.	Excess time required to extract and summarize information.
Condition 8—Input Rules Too Restrictive or Bypassed		
Input rules that are too restrictive may lose data that has important meaning. Data entry clerks may skip entering data into a field (missing information) or arbitrarily change a value to conform to rules and pass an edit check (erroneous information).	Purchase or develop new entry system with excessive edit checks. Noticeable increase in number of data quality instances.	Information is lost, distorted, or unreliable.

Intervention Actions	Target State	Improved Data Use
Condition 6—Complex Data Representations		
Provide appropriate procedures to achieve analyzable representation of non-numeric data.	Analyzable representation.	All types of data are interpretable, understandable, and available for analysis.
Condition 7—Volume of Data		
Gather requirements precisely. Balance additional storage over additional query time and speed to make decisions. Organize data for easy retrieval and use (e.g., digital, graphic information). Provide data categories and contexts. Provide preaggregated data to reduce time to access or aggregate.	Well-organized, relevant data.	Data consumers make timely use of well-organized, relevant data.
Condition 8—Input Rules Too Restrictive or Bypassed		
Motivate data collectors and data custodians to understand the effects of good data. Install appropriate measures to audit data. Implement relevant edit routines. Make data collection part of business process.	Valid and complete data collection and storage.	Complete and relevant data are used by data consumers.

Table 6.1
(continued)

Manifestations	Warning Signs	Impact of Problem
Condition 9—Changing Data Needs		
As information consumers' tasks and the organization environment change, the information that is relevant and useful changes. Often how data are categorized and aggregated, not the base source data, changes. The new base source data are not collected by design and thus are missing.	Changes in consumers, consumer tasks, and competitive or regulatory environment of the organization. Data consumers ask for different reports. Data collectors need to collect and enter different data.	Mismatches develop between available information and what is needed for tasks.
Condition 10—Distributed Heterogeneous Systems		
Distributed heterogeneous systems lead to inconsistent definitions, formats, rules, and values.	Data consumers complain about lack of manipulation, flexibility, and consistency.	Information is inconsistent and difficult to access and aggregate.

reputation than the hospital data does. This general sense of the relative quality of sources, however, is not based on factual analysis.

Subjective judgment occurs at both the hospital and the HMO. Using the notes of doctors and nurses about patients, the hospital's medical record coders designate diagnosis and procedure codes and corresponding Disease-Related Group codes for billing. Although the coders are highly trained, some subjectivity remains. Thus, these data are considered to be less *objective* than raw data.

Data production forms also contribute to reducing *objectivity* of data. At the HMO doctors using preprinted forms with checkboxes for specifying procedure codes generate a reduced range of procedures performed as compared to doctors using free-form input. This variance affects the *believability* of the data.

Intervention Actions	Target State	Improved Data Use
Condition 9—Changing Data Needs		
Review data needs periodically. Review the environment. Clearly designate the responsibility for matching the data to future needs. Collect source data and maintain it at the lowest level. Make it easy to reaggregate data.	Data reflect current and future needs of all stakeholders.	Data reflect business needs.
Condition 10—Distributed Heterogeneous Systems		
Institute consistent procedures. Strive to develop standards for global needs while meeting local variations.	Consistent data across distributed systems with controlled variations.	Data from distributed systems are integrated and used by data consumers.

Data Are Not Accessible

Data quality problems of accessibility are characterized by underlying concerns about technical accessibility, data representation issues interpreted by data consumers as accessibility problems, and data volume issues interpreted as accessibility problems.

When an airline moves to a new airport, its computing operations remain at the old airport, with access to data via unreliable data communication lines. Since reservations have priority, the unreliable lines result in inventory data *accessibility* problems. This in turn contributes to the airline's inventory *accuracy* problems because updating has lower priority than other data-related tasks.

A hospital has an *accessibility* data quality concern related to the confidential nature of patient records. Data consumers realize the importance

Table 6.2
Negative Manifestations of the Ten Root Conditions

Condition	Example Case	Patches	Problems with Patches	Eventual Impact on Data
1. Multiple data sources	Hospital's two illness severity assessment procedures yield two values for the same information.	Use only one of the systems. Download one set of information to consumers.	Other purposes for which nonused system was developed are lost.	Data are not used.
2. Subjective judgment in data production	Medical coders use judgment in selecting Disease-Related Group codes.	Add production rules to reduce information variance.	Added rules are complex, subjective, and possibly inconsistent.	Data are not used.
3. Limited computing resources	Unreliable communication lines lead to incomplete information. Shortage of terminals reduces information value.	Provide more computing resources, or consumers pay for their own computing resources.	Computing resource allocation becomes a political process that may lack a rational basis.	Data are not accessible and eventually not used.
4. Security/accessibility trade-off	Patient medical information must be kept secure and confidential, but analysts and researchers need access.	Local solutions to security breaches and accessibility complaints as they occur.	Every situation becomes unique, which increases time to negotiate accessibility.	Data are not accessible and eventually not used.

5. Coded data across disciplines	Medical images and text notes on patient care must be stored and accessed.	Use coding systems to summarize text and various computing algorithms (e.g., CAT scans) to analyze images.	Addresses only part of the problem and may generate new problems (e.g., difficult-to-interpret codes).	Data are not accessible and eventually not used.
6. Complex data representations	Difficulties in analyzing trends in image and text information are difficult to analyze: "Is pneumonia increasingly common in ICU patients?"	Electronically store text and image information.	Electronic storage can be costly on the collection side with limited benefit on the retrieval side.	Data are difficult to use and eventually not used.
7. Volume of data	Multiple-year trend analysis needs over 12 gigabytes of information for each year. Several thousand records out of several million must be analyzed.	Condense information using codes. Create extracted subsets of information as needed without record.	Information consumers have difficulties interpreting codes. Need for further interpretation of information. Not timely for analysis.	Data are not accessible and eventually not used.

Table 6.2
(continued)

Condition	Example Case	Patches	Problems with Patches	Eventual Impact on Data
8. Input rules too restrictive or bypassed	Information is missing because edit checks would not accept it, and it is altered to get edit checks to accept.	Enter information into a nonedited comment field, and move to appropriate field by program patch. Tell entry clerks not to enter incorrect information.	Requires extra programming and more complex information entry.	Data are not used.
9. Changing data needs	The basis for medical reimbursement to hospitals changes, requiring changes in information processes and systems.	Only when mismatch between information needs and available information becomes too large, revise information processes and systems.	Information, processes, and systems lag behind needs of information consumers.	Data are difficult to use and eventually not used.
10. Distributed heterogeneous systems	Different divisions use different formats for Disease-Related Group codes.	Consumers manage extraction from each system and aggregate the information.	Consumers do not understand data and file structures. Creates a burden on consumers.	Data are difficult to use and eventually not used.

of security for patient records but also perceive the necessary permissions as barriers to accessibility. This affects the overall *reputation* and *added value* of this data. In addition, data custodians become barriers to accessibility because they cannot provide data access without approval.

Coded data across disciplines results in concerns about *interpretability* and *understandability* of data. Coding systems for physician and hospital activities at the hospital and the HMO are necessary for summarizing and grouping common diagnoses and procedures. The expertise required to interpret codes, however, becomes a barrier to *accessibility*. These codes are not understandable to most doctors and analysts. At the HMO analyzing and interpreting data across physician groups cause problems because each group uses different coding systems.

Complex data representations, such as medical data in text or image form, also present an *interpretability* problem. Medical records include text written by doctors and nurses, and images produced by medical equipment. These data are difficult to analyze across time for individual patients. Furthermore, analyzing trends across patients is difficult. Thus, data representation becomes a barrier to data *accessibility*. These data are inaccessible to data consumers because it is not in a representation that permits analysis.

Large volume of data makes it difficult to provide relevant data that *adds value* to tasks in a timely manner. For example, an HMO serves hundreds of thousands of patients, who generate several million patient records tracking medical histories. Analyses of patient records usually require weekend data extraction. Companies that purchase an HMO option increasingly demand evaluations of medical practices, resulting in an increased need for these analyses. The pattern of large amounts of data leading to *timeliness* problems is also interpreted as an *accessibility* problem.

Data Are Difficult to Use

We observed three underlying causes of complaints that available data do not support information consumers' tasks: missing (*incomplete*) data, inadequately defined or measured data, and data that could not be appropriately integrated. To solve these data quality problems, projects were initiated to provide relevant data that *adds value* to the tasks of data consumers.

Incomplete data can arise from operational problems. At an airline company incomplete data in inventory transactions contributes to inventory data accuracy problems. Mechanics sometimes fail to record part numbers on work activity forms. Because the transaction data were incomplete, the inventory database cannot be updated. This in turn produces *inaccurate* records. According to one supervisor, the situation is tolerated because "the primary job of mechanics is to service aircraft in a timely manner, not to fill out forms."

The hospital's data are incomplete by design in contrast to the airline's data that are incomplete due to operational problems. The amount of data in the hospital's TRACE database is small enough to be *accessible* and *complete* enough to be *relevant* and *add value* to data consumers' tasks. As a result, data consumers occasionally complain about incomplete data.

Problems arise through integrating data across distributed systems. At an HMO data consumers complain about inconsistent definitions and data representations across divisions. For example, basic utilization measures, such as hospital days per thousand patients, are defined differently across divisions. These problems are caused by autonomous design decisions and different rules of business process in each division.

Transformations of Data Quality Problems

Conventional data quality approaches employ control techniques (e.g., edit checks, database integrity constraints, and program control of database updates) to ensure data quality. These approaches have improved data quality substantially. Attention to information systems control alone, however, does not yield quality data that corresponds to data consumers' broader concerns. Controls on data storage are necessary but not sufficient. Information systems and data quality professionals need to apply process-oriented techniques to the data production process.

Data consumers perceive any barriers to their access to data to be accessibility problems. Conventional approaches treat accessibility as a technical computer systems issue, not as a data quality concern. From data custodians' viewpoint, they have provided access if data are technically accessible. To data consumers, however, accessibility goes beyond technical accessibility. It includes the ease with which they can manipulate the data in a timely fashion to suit their needs.

These contrasting views of accessibility are evident in our studies. For example, advanced forms of data can now be stored as binary large objects (blobs). Although data custodians provide technical methods for accessing this new form of data, data consumers continue to experience the data as inaccessible because their tasks require them to analyze the data the way they analyze traditional record-oriented data. Other examples of differing views of accessibility include (1) data combined across autonomous systems is technically accessible, but data consumers view it as inaccessible because similar data items are defined, measured, or represented differently; (2) coded medical data are technically accessible as text, but data consumers view them as inaccessible because they cannot interpret the codes; and (3) large volumes of data are technically accessible, but data consumers view the data as inaccessible because of excessive accessing time. Data quality professionals must understand the difference between the technical accessibility they supply and the broad accessibility concerns of data consumers. Once this difference is clarified, technologies such as data warehouses can provide a smaller amount of more relevant data, and graphical interfaces can improve ease of access.

Data consumers evaluate data quality relative to their tasks. At any time, the same data may be needed for multiple tasks that require different quality characteristics. Furthermore, these quality characteristics will change over time as work requirements change. Therefore, providing high-quality data implies tracking an ever-moving target. Conventional approaches handle data quality in context using techniques such as user requirements analysis and relational database queries. These conventional approaches do not explicitly incorporate the changing nature of the context in which the task is performed.

Because data consumers perform many different tasks and the data requirements for these tasks change, data quality requires much more than good data requirements specification. Providing high-quality data along the dimensions of value and usefulness relative to data consumers' tasks places a premium on designing flexible systems with data that can be easily aggregated and manipulated. The alternative is constant maintenance of data and systems to meet changing data requirements.

Concluding Remarks

Until recently there has been little awareness of the pervasiveness of information quality problems and their severe financial and operational costs to organizations. These problems were rarely addressed before they developed into crises. When data quality problems became crises, short-term fixes were applied. Rarely were long-term solutions developed and implemented.

With the increasing dependence of organizations on the quality of information for strategic, managerial, and operational decision making, these short-term solutions are no longer a viable approach. Patching is a reactive response. Organizations must learn to recognize the signs of potential problems and proactively develop solutions before the problems arise. This requires knowledge of information production processes and understanding why these processes perform or fail to perform as intended (Lee and Strong, 2004).

In this chapter we presented the anatomy of ten root conditions of data quality problems. Organizations can develop solutions to these problems before they become crises using the templates we provided in this chapter. Organizations that attend to the early warning signs by taking appropriate actions should have a smoother road to achieving high-quality information and maintaining a viable data quality practice.

7

Identifying Root Causes of Data Quality Problems: A Case of a Health Care Organization

In the previous chapter we introduced a set of ten root conditions that can develop into serious data quality problems and traced how they can be manifested in organizations. A manifested problem can be attributable to several different root conditions, and uncovering its cause can be challenging. It must be a proactive undertaking. The ultimate goal is to prevent future occurrences of the problem, not just to eliminate present occurrences.

No one approach is preeminent. What is important is that a rigorous, logical, disciplined, and collaborative approach takes place. In this chapter we present a detailed case study describing the uncovering of the causes of data quality problems at a health care organization. This company used a hypothesis testing and verification approach. In essence, this approach follows the classical scientific method of observe, generate a hypothesis, and test and verify that the hypothesis holds. Overall, the case represents one company's experience. It nevertheless serves as a comprehensive example of how one might address the issues and complexities of achieving high-quality data.

Case Study: Feelwell Health Systems

The name Feelwell Health Systems is fictitious, but the case study is based on an actual company. We introduce the terminology that the company uses because this terminology will be used throughout the case, in particular, those portions of the case that report on interviews with key personnel. Figure 7.1 shows the key terms used in the industry. Feelwell sells policies to customers. A policy contains certain benefits, chosen by the customer. A customer can purchase one or more policies,

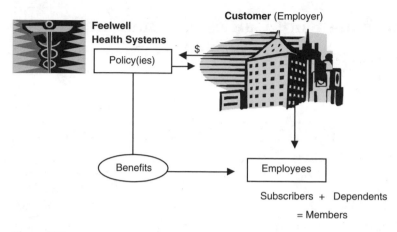

Figure 7.1
Key Terminology

e.g., medical, dental, vision, and so on. Each policy has its own set of benefits. The term *customer* refers to an employer (organization/company) who purchases one or more health care policies for its employees and their dependents. The employees, also known as subscribers, and their dependents are called members. Members consist of subscribers and dependents. A case is primarily made up of information about the customer and its employees and their dependents, policies, contracts, and transactions and processes between the customer and the health care company.

Identifying Problems

At a meeting of stockholders Pauline Brown, the CEO of Feelwell, was reporting a recent $16 million cost saving. Unknown to her, and coincident with the meeting, Karen Arroyo, an information quality manager, discovered data suggesting that Feelwell had unknowingly paid out $16 million in suspect claims over a three-year period. She checked, rechecked, and had others check both the data and the computations. Each iteration yielded the same $16 million figure.

Arroyo plans and directs information quality efforts for the enterprise and especially for PARIS, the enterprise data warehouse. As part of her quality efforts she surveyed the hundreds of internal data warehouse data consumers, followed up the survey with interviews of data customers, and formed a cross-functional team to address issues that might arise. Answers to the survey helped her understand how information problems were affecting the business in general and the customers' work in particular.

The survey and follow-up interviews indicated that the most pressing problems involved information about the cancellation of coverage by the members. A data warehouse customer had first made that discovery and had informed Arroyo that the data warehouse showed more than 41,000 members per month as being active when in fact their policies had been canceled. Arroyo and her group had to address this and other reported problems. On further analysis of the data warehouse, the group found the following:

• 99,490–171,385 members per month were marked as active members for parts of policies when these parts had been canceled.
• Dependents were marked as active when the corresponding subscriber had been canceled.
• Benefit information was missing for members with nonmedical products.
• Surviving spouses were counted twice.
• 45,000–64,000 members who were classified as active had canceled policies.

Arroyo created a control chart of the errors (see figure 7.2) with data points representing 27 consecutive months. The chart showed the number of members whose policies had been canceled but who were still classified as active in the data warehouse. To determine the financial impacts of some of the membership information problems, Arroyo and her group conducted additional analyses that led to the discovery that the claims processing system had paid out $16 million in claims for members whose policies had been canceled.

The survey led Arroyo to immediately interview the benefits manager. A key figure in the case cancellation process, the benefits manager was preparing to transfer to another position. What follows is a portion of Arroyo's interview with the benefits manager, identified in the transcript as CM:

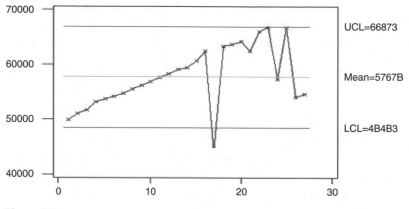

Figure 7.2
Control Chart of "Active" Members Whose Policies Have Been Canceled

KA: In PARIS, 45,000–60,000 members per month show up as active when in fact their policies have been canceled. Would you know why this is happening?

CM: A possible reason might be that CR [Customer Resources] sends notices of cancellations to both CPS [Claims Processing System] and BPS [Benefits Processing System] but CPS cancels at the customer level, not at the member level. The Business Process Improvement team has recommended moving all the cancellation functionality to just one area. Previously, keeping CPS and BPS in synch was a problem. By moving cancellation functions to one area, data can be passed directly to CPS and BPS. A realigned process should happen at the same time—the ball should not be dropped when moving between the new area and Benefits.

KA: Who actually manages this process now?

CM: If I understood correctly, the owner of the member cancellation process is now Customer Relations. If we can find out if the new process is working, a one-shot could be applied to remove past members. I will follow up to ensure that this is happening and to find out the status of the rollout.

KA: I am also seeing active dependents for canceled members. What might you know about that?

CM: CPS has plans to clean that up with a one-shot.

KA: What about future errors?

CM: The data going forward from BPS should not be a problem. A problem was that it was plugged a few years back. The problem is CPS. Currently, data can be entered directly into CPS. A lock-down is planned [we are planning to change the system so that data cannot be entered manually], but there is a lot of push-back from Claims. In addition, reconciliations are being done currently and will be implemented by BPS as first deliverable of next year. I'll contact the project manager of CPS-BPS reconciliation project, which should address this issue.

KA: BPS does not carry information about members with nonmedical-only products. This results in an overstatement of members.

CM: HT [an analyst] is currently looking into that. Nonmedical-only products are no longer being actively marketed, so going forward, we should only see a few exceptions. However, going back and fixing past records would be a major undertaking. An in-depth cost/benefit analysis would be required—it won't be easy to determine where and how much overstatement of members is costing. The other alternative would require new product codes. BPS could handle new product codes, but this would be a major enhancement.

The interview with the benefits manager gave Arroyo a better understanding of the broad picture and the players involved. Feelwell is composed of five segments and the corporate headquarters. The enterprise data warehouse (PARIS), associated department (Enterprise Systems), and Arroyo are part of segment 1. Segment 2 handles the case cancellation process. Segment 3 is also involved in case cancellation. Segment 2 manages BPS and CPS, which both feed data to PARIS. Internal data consumers of the data warehouse span the entire organization.

Some items from the interview proved to be of special interest later in the root cause analysis process:

• "If we can find out if the new process is working, a one-shot could be applied to remove past members. I will follow up to ensure that this is happening and to find out the status of the rollout." "Reconciliations are being done currently and will be implemented by BPS first deliverable of next year." Subsequently Arroyo determined that the new case cancellation process rollout had been delayed by at least several months.

• "The data going forward from BPS should not be a problem ... the CPS-BPS reconciliation project...should address this issue." Unfortunately, it turned out that BPS data going forward was a problem, and the CPS-BPS reconciliation project was put on hold so many times that many doubted it would actually be completed.

• "If we can find out if the new process is working, a one-shot could be applied." "CPS has plans to clean that up with a one-shot." A common response to information quality problems was to perform one-shot fix-ups and reconciliations (a form of data cleansing). Even if these methods had worked, they would have done nothing about root causes, allowing the problems to be masked and to eventually show up again.

Building a Cross-Functional Team

Arroyo recruited team members from the business and technical areas involved in the case cancellation process who represented the three Cs (information collectors, custodians, and consumers). The team formed for a period of six months and met every six weeks. Between team meetings, team members met more frequently in small groups of two or three. Of the multiple problems with membership information, the team chose to begin with the problem of canceled members who were being carried as active in the data warehouse and the costs incurred because of this ($16 million). Considerations of feasibility and financial impact largely dictated the team's choice of issues to study.

Even with the broad representation on the cross-functional team, many challenges remained. For example, an analyst stated, "Identifying reasons why certain problems occur in departments that did not experience the problematic symptoms was akin to digging in one's neighbor's yard to determine why one has a plumbing problem."

Other challenges included the following:

· Time and resources were limited.
· No one person or group knew or understood the entire case cancellation process and all its participants.
· It was difficult to determine who managed which process.
· It was difficult to find needed information and identify who knew what.
· Operating units dealing with the consequences and symptoms felt the pain, but operating units causing the pain did not feel it. Consequently, there was little incentive for further analysis.

Adopting a Framework: Building and Testing Hypotheses

The team used hypothesis building and verification as the basis of its analysis (see figure 7.3). After a few false starts, the team was able to develop causal hypotheses. Once developed, the hypothesis was tested. This process was repeated multiple times until a coherent logic behind the symptoms could be understood and explained. For example, an initial

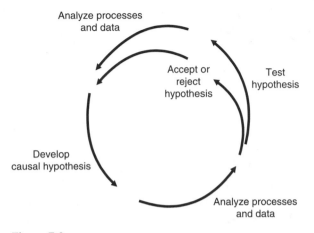

Figure 7.3
Developing and Testing a Hypothesis at Feelwell
Source: Adapted from Katz-Haas and Lee, 2002, p. 21.

assumption was that the claims processing system (CPS) was the problem because CPS had processed and paid the suspect claims; CPS was close to the team in time and space; and the benefits manager felt that CPS was causing the problems. Preliminary investigation, however, pointed to the possibility that problems with the case cancellation process and associated membership information were attributable to multiple causes.

To validate or disprove hypotheses, the team conducted interviews, performed data analyses, tracked records, and asked questions such as "If A were stopped, would the problems be fixed and future problems prevented?" "If B were implemented, would the problem be fixed and future problems prevented?" "If C stopped or started doing this, would it cause other problems? What would the impacts be? Could any negative impacts be mitigated?"

Arroyo and the team understood that a problem is rarely the result of a single factor but rather the result of accumulated decisions, actions, and commitments that become entangled in self-perpetuating workplace dynamics.

Key Information

Membership information is critical to any health care organization. Membership information, including member counts, is used for business analysis of product and service performance, regulatory reporting, and business and financial planning. Member counts are used in a multitude of calculations. When member counts are incorrect, the associated risks affect almost every business process, function, and decision in the company. The risks involved are costly: they include developing workarounds, wasted time in rework, time lost not performing value-added activities, paying claims unnecessarily, inaccurate trending, inadequate member services, programs that are either underfunded or overfunded, missed opportunities, lost customers, inappropriate rates, and poor decisions resulting in lower profit margins.

Membership information is published in various internal and external documents. Errors and inconsistencies can have serious effects on how the company is viewed in the marketplace. In addition, errors in membership information can lead to state and federal regulatory penalties and fines.

Uncovering the Causes of Data Quality Problems

The case cancellation process is triggered by notification from a customer, stating that it will not be renewing its policies with the company. The cancellation information winds its way through departments, functions, business processes, and databases, and is ultimately used for making business decisions, stopping claim payments, calculating member counts, underwriting, creating management reports, and notifying providers.

To uncover causes, the team needed a thorough understanding of these dynamics and the whole cancellation process—both as it was supposed to be and as it was actually practiced. The team began by identifying units, people, and functions involved in the case cancellation process, then subprocesses, databases, and data elements. To uncover information they needed, team members conducted and reconducted interviews with many employees at all levels, gathered documentation, data analysis results, and other artifacts. At the same time, they started looking at those areas and subprocesses that were known to typically cause or permit errors in complex systems, such as functional interfaces, breakdowns in communications, complexity, cycle times/delays, and open feedback loops.

Work practices, organization structures, and the way information systems are developed and deployed are all interdependent but also independent in that none can be reduced to the others. This means that when an information system problem presents itself, it cannot be assumed that the problem is uniquely with the system or even with the system at all.

The mapping process, associated interviews, and several iterations of business process and information flow analysis along with control barrier and causal factor analysis helped unravel relations between information and processes. The team was then able to develop more detailed information product maps and identify some of the "broken places." Figures 7.4 and 7.5 show results from the team's discovery work. The figures represent only a small part of the entire organization.

Note that complexities appear even in these simplified figures. Customer Resources essentially belongs to three departments; Case Install & Cancel (CIC) and Case Setup belong to four. The Customer Portfolio Group is made up of representatives from Benefits, Customer Relations, Customer Portfolio Management, and Customer Resources. Figure 7.5 shows business processes, information processes, and relations between processes, departments, and databases involved in the case cancellation process, and the enterprise data warehouse (PARIS).

To uncover the causes of the problems identified earlier, the team analyzed the collected interview data, meeting memos, e-mails, work documents, observation data, and process flows.

Error Propagation via Unnecessary Process Complexity

The team came to realize how complex the case cancellation process was. A simple process relative to other business processes at Feelwell, it involved 15 departments, 18 subprocesses, 60 third-level processes, 7 systems, 3 of the 5 company segments, and over 300 employees. A number of unnecessary handoffs existed. For example, a Case Install & Cancel analyst filled out part of a required change form and turned it over to a benefits analyst to enter the load date and cancellation reason. The benefits analyst then notified the CIC analyst that the form was complete. The CIC analyst then had to remember to go back into the benefits processing system (BPS) to enter the appropriate data. Without this step, or when there were errors in this step, the feed to propagate cancellations

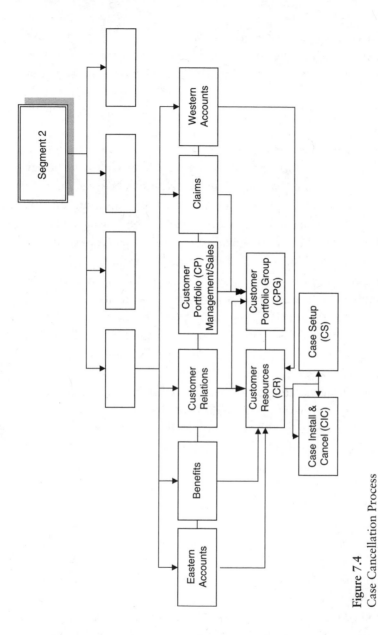

Figure 7.4
Case Cancellation Process

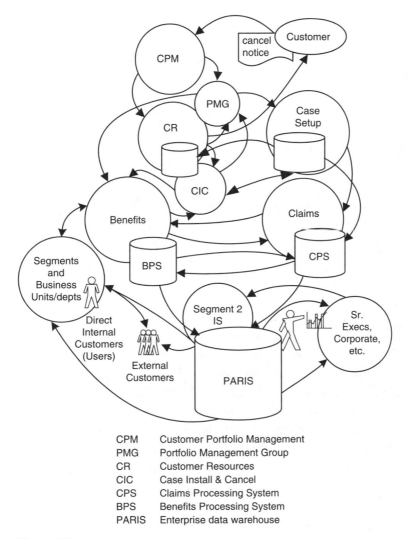

CPM	Customer Portfolio Management
PMG	Portfolio Management Group
CR	Customer Resources
CIC	Case Install & Cancel
CPS	Claims Processing System
BPS	Benefits Processing System
PARIS	Enterprise data warehouse

Figure 7.5
Case Cancellation: Interaction between Information and Business Processes
Source: Adapted from Katz-Haas and Lee, 2002, pp. 24–27.

to the membership level was prevented, and others involved in the process or in downstream processes were unaware of the members who were *not* canceled. The team found that the CIC department was unaware of downstream consequences and costs. Further, information from the original cancellation notification was propagated as data into several different yet parallel flows, causing redundancies and disjoints.

Multiple Sources of Data
A contributing factor to the problems in the claims processing system (CPS) could be traced to Feelwell's corporate history. Feelwell Health Systems was formed via mergers and acquisitions. The latest and largest merger was between a large West Coast company, and another fairly large East Coast company. The East Coast company owned the current claims processing system. This system combined claims data with a robust amount of membership data. The West Coast company owned the benefits processing system. This system was neither robust nor widely used. The East Coast claims processing system eventually became the claims system for the entire company. In exchange, it was decided that the West Coast's benefits processing system would be the company's official benefits processing system. Because both the East Coast and the West Coast systems eventually contained redundant data, disjoints between the two systems began to appear.

BPS contained membership data that did not always match corresponding data from CPS. CPS contained cancellation data that was inconsistent between policy and membership levels. Cases were canceled at different levels in different systems, leading to disjoints. Realignments were run to correct disjoints, but they did not always work.

Poor Screen and Data Formatting
While observing the analysts at work, team members noticed that some of them encountered problems with data entry screens. In data entry screens accelerators allow operators to work more accurately and quickly.

Using BPS data entry screens as an example, problems included text that was all uppercase, which slowed reading and information finding; fields that were not visually or logically organized; difficulties differentiating between field names and the fields themselves; difficulties distinguishing required fields from optional fields; highly cluttered screens; analysts' having to stop data entry to look up codes instead of having these codes easily accessible in an online pick list; fields lacking controls—analysts could easily (albeit accidentally) enter incorrect data.

The case cancellation process contained manual processes such as data entry even in systems that were supposed to be completely automatic. For example, it was necessary to manually go into the customer/coverage record and remove the stop date until data from a customer tape finished loading. Once the tape was complete, it was then necessary to manually reenter the stop date, which in turn generated a job ID that retrieved associated membership. Without this step, or when there were errors in this step, membership cancellations would be incomplete.

Interruption of Data Flows and Lack of Data Flow Continuity

BPS could not always propagate the feed to the membership level. When the propagation failed, BPS did not generate error reports—the benefits analyst had to pull this information and cancel any remaining membership. When this step was neglected, all members were not appropriately canceled, and others in this process or in downstream processes were unaware of the situation. The fact that BPS did not generate error reports was not widely known. Consider this excerpt from a conversation between Arroyo, a benefits manager, a customer resources manager, and a case setup manager:

Benefits: One thing I didn't really think about earlier is that there are so many jobs that can be run. Sometimes your job can get bumped. Error reports must be pulled to identify any problems. This is one more area for human intervention and fall out in the process.

Arroyo: Would you know how often this happens or where I could find a report?

Benefits: Can you direct Karen to a report?

Customer Resources: Once a job is completed, CIC gives the job number to Benefits, and they pull and work out the errors. Can you please point Karen to where the error reports are? Thanks.

Case Setup: Are you talking about termination job error reports? There are none. Benefits needs to run a report generator for any remaining membership and terminate them manually. Even more manual steps.

Benefits: Are you saying that a cancel job does not generate an error report? Why not?

Customer Resources: The developers didn't create one because they were confident [they assumed] that there would be no errors.

According to Feelwell's policies and procedures, the benefits department was to inform the portfolio management group when all members relating to a case were canceled. However, this did not always happen. There were no triggers in place to remind the benefits department to do so or controls that would prevent the benefits department from going on to the next step. Other situations contained similar problems. For example, when more tape jobs were run than BPS could handle, some were canceled. Since BPS did not generate error reports, a CIC analyst had to remember to rerun the job the next day. Should the analysts forget to check, there was no trigger to remind them. Hence the membership would not be completely canceled. A consequence was that no one downstream had any way of knowing about the noncanceled members.

Lack of Timely Delivery of Data

The timing of receipt of the cancellation notification from a customer and notification of the cancellation to claims processing was often delayed. Information from a canceled member's claim, with first service date past the policy cancellation date, could arrive in the claims processing system before any related cancellation information.

According to CIC staff, CIC did not always receive notification of cancellations in a timely manner, delaying cancellation updates. The team looked into reasons for these delays.

The customer portfolio management/sales department was supposed to notify the customer resources department and enter the cancellation information into an access database form within three days of receipt of notification. The portfolio/sales people were rewarded (in commissions) for new accounts. Completing the paperwork associated with cancelling a policy was a low priority because it took time away from new account activity.

Sometimes customers canceled their policies only to change their minds later. The customer resources department spent a fair amount of time and effort reinstating these policies. It was generally understood that this department would release cancellation information at least two weeks before the cancellation effective date. However, to prevent a large number of reinstatements for which it lacked resources, it sometimes held onto cancellations for up to one week before the effective date of the cancellation, not realizing the downstream problems caused by this delay. This delay is an example of a local adaptive change that went undocumented and uncommunicated, causing information problems in the organization system.

Concluding Remarks

The problems that Feelwell Health Systems experienced can be related to a number of the root conditions described in chapter 6. For example, the merger of the disparate systems from the East Coast and West Coast operations was a clear case of multiple sources of data causing problems. The problems of poor screen formats exemplify the root condition of complex data representations. The timeliness problem can be related to the changing needs of customers. In this case, some of the changing needs might be transitory, but nevertheless the organization must react to, and possibly anticipate, these changes.

The Feelwell case illustrates the complexity that will be encountered by an organization in attempting to identify data quality problems and discover their causes. As we stated earlier, the effort requires a determined, logical, persistent, and collaborative approach. The end result, however, places the organization on a sounder footing to resolve problems, improve data quality, and foster a continuous data quality improvement program and environment.

8

Managing Information as Product

A key perspective underlying all the material in this book is that information must be managed as product using an information product approach, or IP approach. This is one of the crucial axioms on which the perspectives and policies presented in this book are based. In this chapter we elaborate on this concept, defining it rigorously and examining in detail what managing information as product entails. This chapter serves as a prerequisite to chapter 9, in which a specific methodology based on information product maps (IP-Maps) is covered.

Information Product

The concept of treating information as product was elaborated in an article by Wang et al. (1998). Based on many investigations of information quality problems encountered by organizations, the need for firms to treat information as product, as an end deliverable that satisfies consumer needs, became clear. Contrast this approach to the often observed treatment of information as by-product. The by-product approach places its focus on the wrong target, usually the system instead of the end product, the information.

Here we refine the general definition of an information product. In order to do so, we first must define the concept of a data element. A data element is the smallest unit of named data that has meaning in the context of the operational environment. A data element could be, for example, an attribute in an entity, a field in a record, or a form. Note that smallest unit must be interpreted in context. Date of birth, social security number, and name are examples of data elements, while 1 March 1985,

026-345-6723, and John Doe are instances of each of the three data elements.

We define an information product (IP) as a collection of data element instances that meets the specified requirements of a data consumer. Such requirements could be needed for business decision making, legal reporting, or government reporting. An example of an IP is a birth certificate.

Managing information as product requires a fundamental change in understanding information. To properly treat information as product, a company must follow four principles:

• Understand the consumer's information needs.
• Manage information as the product of a well-defined production process.
• Manage information as a product with a life cycle.
• Appoint an information product manager to manage the information product.

Application of this set of principles is the information product (IP) approach. It is the keystone on which the delivery of consistent information quality depends. In the next section we use four cases to illustrate the IP approach, lay out the argument in support of the IP approach, highlight some of the negative consequences of not using the approach, and provide a framework that will aid management in implementing an IP approach.

Four Cases

The four cases in this section represent diverse enterprises. In total, however, they illustrate the four principles of the IP approach (see figure 8.1) and the negative consequences that can result when the IP approach is not applied.

Financial Company is a leading investment bank with extensive domestic and international operations. Its customers need to trade immediately after opening a new account. The new account has to be linked to accounts the customer may have opened, and the information in all accounts has to be accurate, up-to-date, and consistent. The bank requires real-time account balance information in order to enforce minimum account balance rules across a customer's multiple accounts. Failures in this area of operations expose the company to potentially large

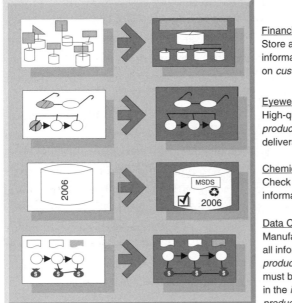

Financial Company
Store and manufacture
information product based
on *customers'* needs.

Eyewear Company
High-quality information
production process
delivers high-quality lenses.

Chemical Company
Check *life cycle* of its
information product.

Data Company
Manufacturing cost from
all information
production processes
must be accounted for
in the *information
product.*

Figure 8.1
Case Studies in Managing Information as Product

monetary losses. By statute, the company has to close all the accounts of
a customer when informed by federal authorities of criminal activities on
the part of the customer. Adhering to the statute requires timely, integrated information on a customer's accounts.

Eyewear Company sells eyewear products at its retail outlets throughout the country. The retail outlets generate specifications for the eyewear
products and forward them to lens grinders at one of four laboratories.
The laboratory receives over 25,000 eyeglass orders each week. The ability to produce eyeglasses that meet consumer needs depends heavily on
the quality of information provided to the grinders at the laboratories.
If the grinder's information needs are not met, the production of lenses
is adversely affected.

Chemical Company, a Fortune 500 company, is a major presence in
the petrochemical industry. For each chemical product, Chemical Company is legally required to produce a material safety data sheet (MSDS)
that identifies the potential hazards of the product, the symptoms of
the hazard, and the actions to be taken should a symptom be observed.

Because of the extremely high product liability costs of not reporting potential hazards, the company has every incentive to provide accurate, complete, timely, and understandable safety data sheets. Chemical Company has a well-defined process for creating the sheets. When a new chemical is developed, the MSDS group contacts experts who contribute to the specification of the MSDS.

Data Company captures data from hundreds of millions of transactions a week generated by tens of thousands of retail stores. Clients purchase information that is refined from the raw data collected from these retail stores. Data Company had built sufficient intelligence into its systems to provide high-quality information. It has been using neural networks for several years and has built an imputation process that estimates any missing data. For example, this system enables the company to correct data that is corrupted by failed or bad transmissions. What the company does not do is pay proper attention to its own information production process. This causes problems when it prices its products.

Four Principles

1. Understand information consumers' needs.
Financial Company and Eyewear Company have to determine the needs of two types of information consumer: the external customer and the internal consumer. Each company provides an example of what can happen when a business fails to understand those needs.

For its external customers, Financial Company must open new accounts quickly, maintain up-to-date customer risk profiles, and know all accounts related to a particular customer. Investments at inappropriate customer risk levels cause major customer dissatisfaction and potential indemnification to customers for losses. For its internal consumers, Financial Company must provide real-time information about any changes in customers' account balances. Not doing so causes different internal consumers to use locally maintained databases that often are inconsistent.

Satisfying the needs of Eyewear's customers translates into providing the proper lenses, which depends on the retail outlet's sending the correct lens specifications to the laboratory. When the opticians, the writers of the specifications, misunderstand the information needs of the lens grinders (the internal information consumers), the result is that many lenses need to be reworked. Often, special instructions from the optician to the grinder are not communicated properly and do not meet the information needs of the grinder. Regrinding lenses leads to additional costs and delays that lower external customer satisfaction.

2. Manage information as the product of a well-defined information production process.

Financial Company maintains a centralized customer account database. Every night it posts transactions that occur throughout the day and updates customer account balances. Other customer information, such as the customer's risk profile, however, is updated on an ad hoc basis, when convenient. This ad hoc approach results from treating information solely as a by-product of a physical event rather than as the product of a well-defined information production process. A change would be triggered by, for example, a customer request. A well-defined production process, in this context, would require systematic examination of customer behavior and the attendant updating of the risk profile.

Financial Company's internal consumers view customer account information as unreliable. One vice president joked, "Everyone but the consultant has updating privilege to customer account information." To solve these problems, individual departments develop individual customer account databases. The result is a proliferation of local customer databases with inconsistencies among them. These local databases are tailored to the specific needs of each department and contain more current information on the department's customers than the central database does. Each department collects and processes information as a by-product of its local operations, independent of the corporation's need for integrated customer account information.

3. Manage the life cycle of information product.

In adapting the classical marketing notion, we define the information product life cycle as the stages through which information passes from introduction to obsolescence. The life cycle can be divided into four stages: introduction (creation), growth, maturity, and decline. Chemical Company is an example of an organization that does not follow this principle. Its well-defined process for creating safety sheets does not extend to maintaining the quality of this information over the life cycle of the information product. As a result, information on new hazards, based on accumulated experience with the product and emerging scientific evidence, is incorporated into a product's safety sheet erratically. Over time information quality deteriorates.

At Financial Company changes in the operating environment call for updated production processes to improve the company's information products. Financial Company, however, does not manage the life cycle of its customer account information to accommodate the new global, legal, and competitive environment, resulting in potentially huge problems for the bank. It is not poised to leverage customer account information in its global operations. For example, customers with sufficient credit across accounts cannot trade or borrow on their full balances. Tracking customer balances for individual and multiple accounts, closing all accounts of a customer because of criminal activities, and ensuring an accurate customer risk profile also cannot be accomplished without significant error-prone human intervention.

4.   Appoint an information product manager to manage information processes and products.

We use the term information product manager to represent a generic functional role in the organization. Different companies use different terms or titles depending on the scope of responsibility and position in the firm's management hierarchy. At Financial Company, an information product manager would be responsible for monitoring and capturing customer needs continually, reconciling those varied needs, and transforming the knowledge into a process of continual improvement. Without an such a manager Financial Company establishes few information process measures or controls. For example, the bank has no controls to ensure that customer risk profiles are regularly updated. It does not standardize or inspect the account creation process. As a result, it establishes no metrics to determine how many accounts are created on time and whether customer information in those accounts is updated. Because management gives its attention to revenue-generating operations such as trading, the information technology department finds itself responding reactively to ad hoc requests from the trading department for updated customer account information. If Financial Company appointed an information product manager, it would enjoy better risk management and customer service—two critical success factors for companies in the financial industry.

Financial Company began a transition to an IP perspective in the early 1990s by hiring a new information technology director who was knowledgeable about information quality concepts, process engineering, and business applications. The director began to institute a cross-functional approach. With support from the CEO, he constructed a work flow model of the customer account information production process that integrated client services, business operations, and the information department. The process of producing high-quality customer account information then began.

Managing Information as By-product Will Not Work

Managers can always view and manage information as a by-product of a system or event. From the perspective of the people using the information, however, it is a product, not a by-product. In contrasting the by-product approach to the information-as-product approach, there are five factors to analyze: what is managed, how is it managed, why manage it, what is considered success, and who manages it (see table 8.1).

What Is Managed?
Organizations often focus inappropriately on managing the life cycle of the hardware and software that produce the information instead of on the information itself. As a result, they fail to capture the additional knowledge necessary to achieve meaningful information quality. For example, in Eyewear Company the grinding instructions were distinct from, and just as important as, the actual lenses. If the instructions were not correct, the lenses would not be correct. In the course of selling the eyeglasses to the customer, the focus should be on the form in which the information is delivered to the grinder, not on the system that captures and transmits the information.

How Is Information Product Managed?
In the by-product approach, because the organization's focus is on the life cycle of hardware and software systems, the means of producing

Table 8.1
Managing Information as Product vs. By-product

	Information as Product	Information as By-product
What is managed?	Information; information product life cycle	Hardware and software; systems life cycle
How is it managed?	Integrated, cross-functional approach that encompasses information collectors, custodians, and consumers	Integrate stove-pipe systems; control individual components; control costs
Why manage it?	Deliver high-quality information to consumers	Implement high-quality hardware and software system
What is success?	Deliver high-quality information continuously over the product life cycle; no GIGO (garbage in, garbage out)	The system works; no bugs
Who manages it?	Chief information officer (CIO); information product manager	CIO; information technology director and database administrators

Source: Adapted from Wang et al., 1998, p. 98.

information become ends in themselves. Managers focus on individual components of the systems and attempt to establish cost controls on those components. They view these components in isolation from one another instead of treating them as an integrated whole.

The situation at Eyewear Company demonstrates what can happen when the organization focuses primarily on components. When asked for lens rework figures, the information technology director stated, "We know we have 15 percent errors." Left unstated was the assumption that the errors were attributed to the grinding machines. All attention was on the hardware and software components of the lens production, not on information for the lens specification. It took outside observers to recognize that communication problems between opticians and grinders led to the higher error rate. Many problems resulted from mismatches between how opticians wrote orders and how grinders read these orders. For example, the opticians used special instruction lines on the form to add information. The grinders ignored that information because they did not expect grinding specifications there. The information technology department also contributed to the problem. The director primarily focused on hardware and software upgrades and did not pay sufficient attention to how each function interpreted the information being transmitted. No one held a cross-functional perspective.

Failing to treat lens specifications as an information product resulted in additional work of regrinding approximately 40,000 lenses per year. The problem was costing the company more than $1 million annually in rework expenses as well as other costs such as those associated with customer dissatisfaction. Eyewear Company was not treating the opticians and grinders, in their roles as information collectors and consumers, as part of one integrated system.

Financial Company provides another example of a misplaced focus on individual components. Databases were optimized at the local level and not truly integrated. The account managers, who were the internal information consumers, had local information for local needs. But they did not have access to the integrated, global information required to exploit emerging opportunities. The partial information that account managers received hindered their ability to manage risk, improve service, and increase revenue.

Why Manage Information as Product?

Too often, the information technology department emphasizes improving the quality of the delivery system and its components rather than improving the quality of the information product delivered to consumers. The latter approach requires a thorough knowledge of consumers' information needs and quality criteria.

Eyewear Company illustrates the undue and misplaced emphasis on component improvement. The special instruction section of the order forms was supposed to improve the order-writing component but did nothing to improve the quality of information supplied to the grinders. This made the opticians' task easier at the information consumers' (grinders') expense.

In contrast, Data Company was rapidly evolving toward managing information as product. It was beginning to manage the entire information delivery process as an integrated system. It adopted a companywide Total Data Quality Management (TDQM) program and invested in modernizing its technology infrastructure. The company worked with its information collectors to produce better information. It instituted procedures that enabled information consumers to report information quality problems directly. Because the company tailored its information products to individual clients, it recognized the need to proactively partner with its clients.

Even with all this attention to an integrated production process, some communication problems remained. For example, Data Company had problems pricing its products because fixed costs were not communicated well within the company. The cost data was accurate, but it was not represented in a manner usable by the marketing department. For example, data such as management overhead was not appropriately communicated to the sales force. As a result, Data Company's sales force did not trust the information technology department's cost data and continued to ignore the management overhead in contract bid pricing. This situation prompted the marketing executive vice president to state, "I may not price strictly based on cost, but I need to know the cost." The company's profit margins remained low despite its predominant position in a competitive market. One reason that a company manages information as product is to avoid such problems by ensuring that everyone understands the purpose behind the need for information.

What Is Success?

Treating information as product instead of as by-product changes the measures of success. Rather than judging the success of the computer system based on its having no "bugs," companies measure their success by the information's fitness for consumer use. Focusing on the computer system reflects a short-term perspective. The initial information may be produced without error, but little attention is given to changes occurring later in the product life cycle.

Chemical Company's experience with the deteriorating quality of its safety sheets over time provides an example of failure to recognize the need to deliver high-quality information product to consumers over a product's life cycle. As the company's chemical products were used, evidence of new hazards arose from cumulated experience in using the products and from new scientific discoveries. The company was expected to update its safety sheets as new evidence became available. It often failed to do so. Chemical Company measured its success by the high quality of its initial safety information. The life cycle of the information, however, is not necessarily the same as the life cycle of the chemical product. A truer measure of success would account for this difference and assess the quality of the safety information over its life cycle.

Who Manages Information Product?

If companies take an information product approach and manage across functions, they must adopt a management structure for this environment by appointing an information product manager. This position is not identical to that of chief information officer (CIO). The CIO oversees the management of the firm's data repositories, among other responsibilities. The database administrator, a subordinate function reporting to the CIO, directly manages the repositories. In the four cases discussed earlier, solutions to information quality problems required management intervention. Our research suggests that the person doing the intervening should not be the database administrator, whose traditional focus has been to control what enters the databases. This function does not typically focus on the production and delivery of information as a cross-functional, integrated system involving information collectors, custodians, and consumers.

What was striking about the four companies is their intuitive sense that they needed an information product manager. Each had an individual performing the duties that we would associate an information product manager's, although they did not use that designation. They took an information product view and began to manage information with that in mind.

Concluding Remarks

In this chapter we elaborated on the concept of treating and managing information as product. We gave a formal definition of information product and presented a set of principles and prescriptions to manage information as product. The function of information product manager was introduced. In chapter 9 we introduce a specific modeling formalism, information product maps, or IP-Maps. This approach is still under development, but even in its present state it has proved effective in helping manage information as product. We touched on a variation of this approach in chapter 2 in the discussion of the value proposition for data quality.

9

Developing Information Product Maps

To implement the information product (IP) approach, an organization needs not only a supportive philosophy but also models, tools, and techniques. In earlier chapters we discussed a number of ways in which an organization can foster data quality awareness and identify root causes. These methods are part of the tool kit of the information product manager and data quality analysts. These in conjunction with the construct of information product maps provide a formidable set of tools to implement the IP approach and support a viable data quality program.

It is important to make clear at the outset that the development of a standard methodology for producing IP-Maps is an ongoing project and that the ideas and constructs presented here are evolving. Nevertheless, the constructs are usable and useful. Work is ongoing to establish standards for the creation and maintenance of information product maps. An ad hoc committee of academics and data quality practitioners has been working to establish these standards. We refer to this committee as Standards Group throughout this chapter.

Basic Definitions, Concepts, and Symbols

To begin, we reiterate the basic definitions of data element and information product that were introduced in chapter 8. A data element is the smallest unit of named data that has meaning in the context of the operational environment. An information product is a collection of data element instances that meets the specified requirements of a data consumer.

This definition of information product is consistent with the intuitive or implicit meaning of *information product* used in previous research. It serves as a general definition that can be used by anyone working in the area of information product maps.

Standards Group, Committee on Information Product Maps, has suggested a preliminary set of symbols and constructs with which to construct IP-Maps. The committee's work is based on research by Ballou et al. (1998), Shankaranarayan, Ziad, and Wang (2003), and Wang et al. (2002) which we also draw on here.

An IP-Map is a systematic representation of the process involved in manufacturing or creating an information product. It uses a standard set of symbols and conventions. The standards group identifies four forms of information product:

• *Standard type.*   IPs that have prespecified formats and that are generated periodically on a schedule or that can be produced on demand if necessary. Typical business reports, billing statements, and pay stubs are examples.

• *Ad hoc type.*   These are entities of flexible format that are not predefined. They are created on demand and customized at the time of need.

• *Storage type.*   These consist of physically meaningful collections of records, files, and databases.

• *Free format type.*   These include meaningful collections of data whose format is not rigidly predefined. They include data from nontext media such as video and audio, and also from print media such as books and periodicals.

To improve the quality of the various types of information product may require diverse tactics. Each type, however, is an information product and can be subjected to the methodology and mapping conventions presented here.

At present the standard set of symbols and conventions is evolving. But even in its present state it is usable for depicting the creation of an information product. Table 9.1 lists the basic symbols that are used to construct IP-Maps. Each block gives a definition of the construct, the symbol used to represent it, and some examples. As IP-Maps are increasingly used, and new knowledge is gained, the set of symbols will be modified.

There are some similarities between IP-Maps and data flow diagrams. Any time one deals with flows and transformation of data, similarities in the diagramming techniques arise. An IP-Map is more than simply a data

Table 9.1
IP-Map Guide

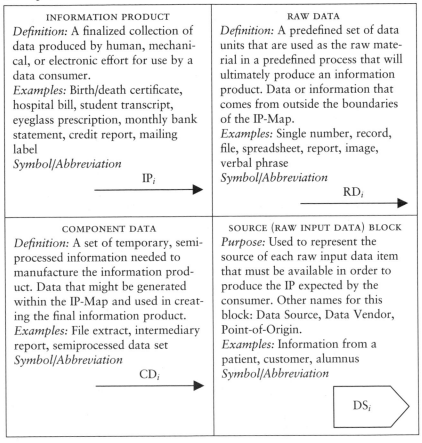

INFORMATION PRODUCT	RAW DATA
Definition: A finalized collection of data produced by human, mechanical, or electronic effort for use by a data consumer. *Examples:* Birth/death certificate, hospital bill, student transcript, eyeglass prescription, monthly bank statement, credit report, mailing label *Symbol/Abbreviation* IP_i ⟶	*Definition:* A predefined set of data units that are used as the raw material in a predefined process that will ultimately produce an information product. Data or information that comes from outside the boundaries of the IP-Map. *Examples:* Single number, record, file, spreadsheet, report, image, verbal phrase *Symbol/Abbreviation* RD_i ⟶
COMPONENT DATA	SOURCE (RAW INPUT DATA) BLOCK
Definition: A set of temporary, semiprocessed information needed to manufacture the information product. Data that might be generated within the IP-Map and used in creating the final information product. *Examples:* File extract, intermediary report, semiprocessed data set *Symbol/Abbreviation* CD_i ⟶	*Purpose:* Used to represent the source of each raw input data item that must be available in order to produce the IP expected by the consumer. Other names for this block: Data Source, Data Vendor, Point-of-Origin. *Examples:* Information from a patient, customer, alumnus *Symbol/Abbreviation* DS_i ⟩

flow diagram, however. The IP-Map includes much more information than is found on a data flow diagram or an entity relationship diagram. Information on information collectors, custodians, and consumers should be included. Specific information on the degree of participation and the roles of these stakeholders in the production process should be noted. Information on the system infrastructure, organization infrastructure, and specific functions and responsibilities should be spelled out. An important aspect of IP-Maps is that they incorporate information on data quality dimensions. Ballou et al. (1998) have shown how data quality dimensions, particularly timeliness, can be incorporated into some of the blocks of the IP-Map.

Table 9.1
(continued)

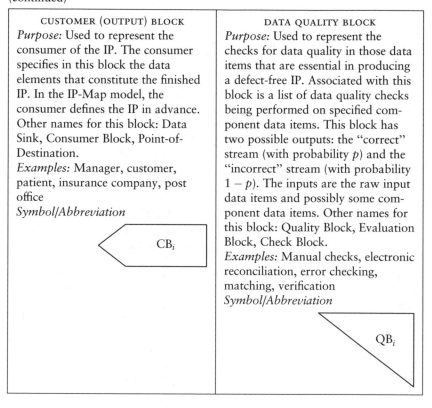

CUSTOMER (OUTPUT) BLOCK	DATA QUALITY BLOCK
Purpose: Used to represent the consumer of the IP. The consumer specifies in this block the data elements that constitute the finished IP. In the IP-Map model, the consumer defines the IP in advance. Other names for this block: Data Sink, Consumer Block, Point-of-Destination. *Examples:* Manager, customer, patient, insurance company, post office *Symbol/Abbreviation*	*Purpose:* Used to represent the checks for data quality in those data items that are essential in producing a defect-free IP. Associated with this block is a list of data quality checks being performed on specified component data items. This block has two possible outputs: the "correct" stream (with probability p) and the "incorrect" stream (with probability $1 - p$). The inputs are the raw input data items and possibly some component data items. Other names for this block: Quality Block, Evaluation Block, Check Block. *Examples:* Manual checks, electronic reconciliation, error checking, matching, verification *Symbol/Abbreviation*

Procedure to Generate an IP-Map

The procedure to generate an IP-Map captures the essence of the initial proposals of Standards Group. The group's suggestions are presented as methods for identifying, mapping, prioritizing, and improving the quality of an organization's information products. Here we concentrate on the steps involved in creating one IP-Map.

• *Step 1.*   Choose the IP to be mapped. Choose the data elements that constitute the basic building blocks of the IP. This is accomplished in different ways depending on the situation. In one case, the data elements are obtained by examining and decomposing the IP. In another case, it may be that an explicit IP cannot be clearly identified or described. Then a bottom-up approach can be used by choosing one or more data

Table 9.1
(continued)

PROCESSING BLOCK	DECISION BLOCK
Primary Purpose: Used to represent manipulations, calculations, or combinations involving some or all raw input data items or component data items required to produce the IP. *Secondary Purpose:* Used as a data correction block. When errors are identified in a set of data elements that enter the data quality block, some corrective action is required. This block represents a process that is not part of the standard processing sequence but is utilized under special circumstances. Any raw input data items or component data items that go through the correction block can be considered cleansed and used by subsequent blocks without needing to return to the data quality block. Other names for this block: Process Block, Data Correction Block. *Examples:* Updates, edits, data capture, uploads, downloads, report creation, file creation *Symbol/Abbreviation* P_i	*Purpose:* In some complex information manufacturing systems, depending on the value of particular data items, it may be necessary to direct some data items to a different set of blocks downstream for further processing. In such cases, a decision block is used to capture the different conditions to be evaluated and the corresponding procedures for handling the incoming data items based on the evaluation. *Examples:* The same set of birth-related data items may be used to generate a birth certificate, a summary report of vital statistics, or a report to accompany the blood sample from a newborn to test for congenital diseases. *Symbol/Abbreviation* D_i

elements that appear critical to the IP. The set of data elements can later be refined (elements added and removed) as the map is developed.

• *Step 2.*   Identify the data collector, the data custodian, and the data consumer. It is important to identify who is creating, collecting, and entering the data; who is responsible for maintaining the data; and who will use the data.

• *Step 3.*   Depict the IP by capturing the flows of the data elements, their transformations, and the connections between and among flows.

Table 9.1
(continued)

DATA STORAGE BLOCK	INFORMATION SYSTEM BOUNDARY BLOCK
Purpose: Used to represent the capture of data items in storage files or databases so that they can be available for further processing. Storage blocks may be used to represent data items (raw or component) that wait for further processing or are captured as part of the information inventory. Other names for this block: Data Block, Information Storage Block. *Examples:* Database, file system *Symbol/Abbreviation* STO_i	*Purpose:* Used to reflect the changes to raw input data items or component data items as they move from one type of information system to another. These system changes could be intra- or inter-business units. *Example:* Data entry from paper to electronic form *Symbol/Abbreviation* SB_i
BUSINESS BOUNDARY BLOCK	INFORMATION SYSTEM–BUSINESS BOUNDARY BLOCK
Purpose: Used to represent instances where raw input data items or component data items are handed over by one organization unit to another. Used to specify the movement of IP (or raw input or component data items) across department or organization boundaries. Other names for this block: Organization Boundary Block. *Example:* Data transfer from surgical unit to patient unit *Symbol/Abbreviation* BB_i	*Purpose:* Defined for circumstances where raw input data items or component data items go through both business boundary and system boundary changes. Other names for this block: Information System–Organization Boundary Block, Information System–Organization Combo Block. *Examples:* Data transfer from Windows NT in patient care department to IBM RS/6000 Cluster in administration; change from admission unit's RDC Ultrix to IBM RS/6000 Cluster in administration *Symbol/Abbreviation* BSB_i

• *Step 4.* Identify the functional roles. Identify the pertinent systems. Identify the individuals involved and their respective responsibilities.

The information can now be incorporated into the map. Generally, this sequence would be followed:

• Draw the physical flow/work flow.
• Draw the data flow.
• Draw systems infrastructures.
• Draw organization infrastructure and roles.

Further, an inventory of the collection of information product (Pierce, 2005) can enhance managing information. We now turn to the notational conventions of IP-Maps and illustrate them with appropriate examples.

Building the IP-Map: A Case Example

In this section we describe the generation of IP-Maps for important information products used in a hospital. The case is taken from previous research (Shankaranarayan, Ziad, and Wang 2003). We limit ourselves to a small subset of the operations and processes of a major hospital, including only the in-patient admissions, treatment, and discharge sections.

There are five products associated with these operations. All five use information that is gathered from two important sources: the patient and the team of hospital employees (doctors, nurses, lab technicians, radiologists, therapists, and administrative staff) involved directly or indirectly in the admission, treatment, or discharge of the patient. Each uses a subset of the large set of information. The first product (IP_1) is the *admissions report*, submitted to the management of the hospital on a daily, weekly, and monthly basis. It provides a description of the number of patients admitted, expected duration of stay, and patient information, and it serves as a monitoring instrument that reflects how busy the units are. The second product (IP_2) is the *patient treatment report*, generated on a daily basis and appended to the patient's chart. Care providers (nurses/doctors) use it to monitor the patient's response(s) to treatments and procedures. These two are information products used internally by the hospital. The final three products are sent to external agencies. The *birth/death report* (IP_3) is submitted to the registry of vital statistics, and the *health report* (IP_4) is a biannual report required by the department of public health on the types of patients treated and released, ailments, treatments, and the reason for discharge. The final product (IP_5) is the *patient bill* submitted to the health maintenance organizations (HMOs) for payment. This is an itemized list of services, equipment charges (if any), medications, tests, and procedures provided to the patient.

The IP-Map representing the manufacture of the patient admission report (IP_1) is shown in figure 9.1. An in-patient may be admitted at any one of three locations: the admissions office, the emergency room, or the department of maternal and fetal medicine. The patient (or an accompanying adult) provides the patient information (raw data RD_1 from data source DS_1) by completing a form. The admissions clerk enters this data into the patient medical office system using a form-based interface (process P_1). In this process the data changes from a paper-based system to an electronic system, shown by the system boundary block SB_1. The software module associated with the interface checks the form for completeness and verifies the guarantor/HMO; this check is shown as QB_1. The raw data elements examined along with the authorization, shown by the component data CD_1, are sent for storage.

Upon admission, the ward nurse responsible for admitting the patient assigns a bed number that specifies the type of ward (cardiac intensive care unit, general); she also examines the general condition and disposition of the patient. The nurse (treated as two data sources, DS_3 and DS_4, because the two tasks may be done by more than one nurse) records this information (RD_3 and RD_4) on the chart and enters it into the computer system (process blocks P_3 and P_4). Because the underlying system changes, a system boundary block (SB_3) is shown to represent this change. The patient's past medical records (source block DS_2) are obtained, and the information (RD_2) is used to update the patient's medical record in the system (process P_2). The records are verified to ensure that they come from the right source authorized by the patient, and if necessary the information is verified with the doctor/medical office that created the record. Quality block QB_2 represents this check. The resulting component data (CD_2) is then sent for storage. All of this information is captured in the data storage of the medical office system, shown by the storage block STO_1. The information product IP_1, generated by

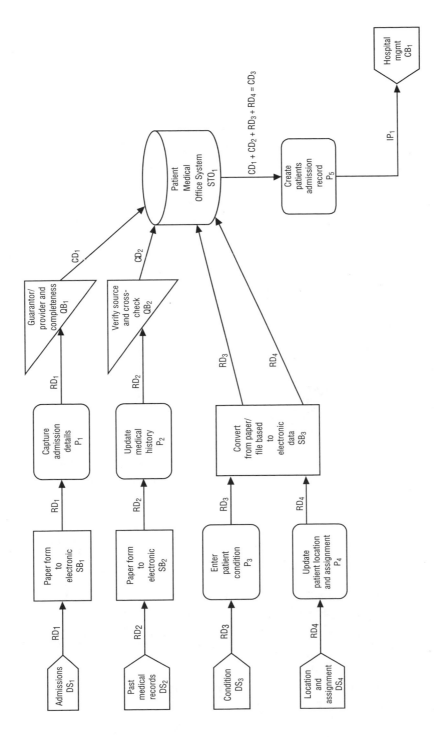

Figure 9.1
IP-Map for Patient Admission Record
Source: Adapted from Wang et al., 2003.

process P_5, uses a collection of component data items cumulatively identified as CD_3. It is sent to the hospital management, as shown by the consumer block CB_1.

Once the admission is complete, a record of the treatments/procedures recommended and performed is created, as shown by the IP-Map in figure 9.2. The specialists and attending physicians (data sources DS_7 and DS_8) recommend the course of treatment and procedures/tests to be performed. This information is then recorded (RD_7) on the charts. Prior to its capture, it is verified by the attending physicians and modified (if needed) in consultation with the specialist. The quality block QB_4 represents this check. The resulting authorized treatments/procedure information (CD_5) is captured in the computer system by process P_8. The attending physicians also report on the progress of the patient and sign off on the recommended treatments/procedures completed, as shown by RD_8, which is captured in the system by process P_9. The change of system from paper-based to electronic is represented by SB_5. The reports from the labs and radiology (data source DS_5) are collected and the information (RD_5) is entered into the computer. The change in system is represented by SB_4. Process P_6 captures this, and a module in this process verifies the source of the report as well. The component data CD_4, generated by P_6, is matched with the patient's record, shown by QB_3, and sent for storage.

The comments and reports from the surgical unit (different from the patient care facility) are electronically uploaded by process P_7. The business boundary block BB_1 represents the transfer of information across business units. The storage location for all this information is the patient care system database, shown by storage block STO_2. The treatment report (IP_2) is created by process P_{10} and sent to caregivers (customer block CB_2).

The manufacture of the information products IP_3, IP_4, and IP_5 is represented by the IP-Map in figure 9.3. The information in the admissions office system and the patient care system is uploaded into the administrative system by processes P_{11} and P_{12}. The records from each are matched to ensure that the right admission is combined with the right treatment (shown by quality block QB_6), and the resulting component data CD_{10} is stored in the administrative system database, represented by STO_3. Because all three systems are different, we need to show the change in the

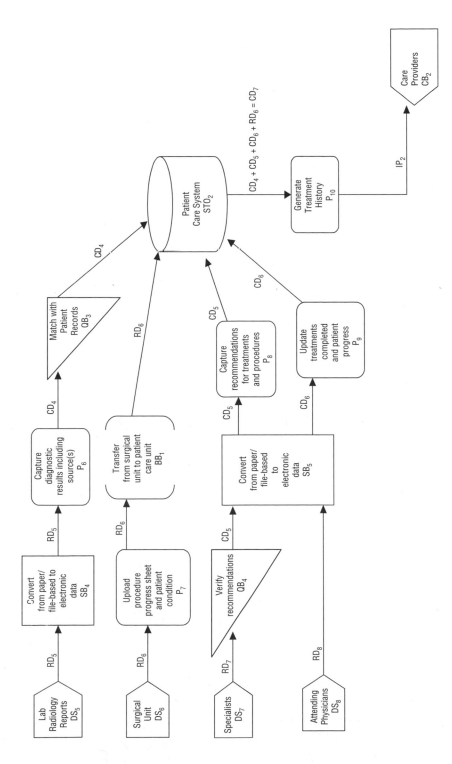

Figure 9.2
IP-Map for Patient's Treatment History
Source: Wang et al., 2003.

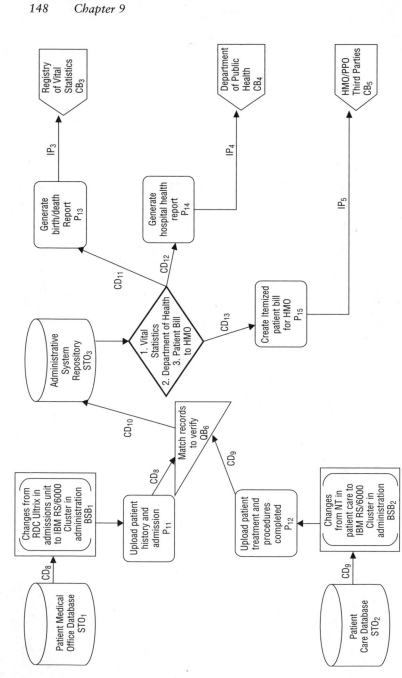

Figure 9.3
IP-Map for Vital Statistics Report, Hospital Health Report, and Bill
Source: Wang et al., 2003.

Table 9.2
Sample Metadata for the IP-Map in Figure 9.1

Name/Type	Department/ Role	Location	Business Process	Composed of Base System
Admissions —DS_1	Admissions office/patient	Admissions, OB/GYN, emergency room	Standard form (#1101P)	Paper-based— patient file
Past medical records— DS_2	Admissions office/ admissions clerk	Admissions building, records room	Contact source and request with patient authorization	Paper-based— patient file

Source: Wang et al., 2003.

underlying system during this transfer. We also need to capture the fact that the information changes business boundaries. We use the combined system and business boundary blocks BSB_1 and BSB_2 to represent the transfer. Process P_{13} generates the report on vital statistics (IP_3), which is sent to the consumer (CB_3) and the Registry of Vital Statistics. Processes P_{14} and P_{15} generate the hospital health report (IP_4) and the patient bill (IP_5), respectively. The state department of health (CB_4) and the HMO (CB_5) are the consumers of the two information products. The set of data items used to generate each product is different and is shown by the component data items CD_{11}, CD_{12}, and CD_{13}.

To complete the representation, we need to capture the information about each of the blocks and the data elements included in each flow in the model(s). This is akin to the data dictionary for a data flow diagram, and we refer to this as the metadata associated with the model. The metadata is captured in a repository. The complete metadata for the model is too large to be shown here, and therefore only a sample is shown in table 9.2.

Concluding Remarks

In this chapter we introduced the concept of the information product map, or IP-Map. We presented a set of symbols and diagrammatic conventions with which to build the maps. Development of IP-Maps is a relatively new endeavor, and the symbols and conventions are still evolving. Nevertheless, the rendering of these IP-Maps is integral to assessing, diagnosing, and conveying the quality of data to individuals in the organization. The maps become indispensable tools in diagnosing data quality problems. In most organizations no one person or group has complete knowledge about all processes, systems, people, and, organization units involved in key sets of information product. Developing and implementing IP-Maps serves as a mechanism to facilitate managing organization knowledge about collecting, storing, maintaining, and using organization data.

10

Data Quality Initiatives: A Case of a Large Teaching Hospital

Having introduced the concept of treating information as a product in chapter 8 and the construct and formalisms of IP-Maps in chapter 9, we now present the case of a large teaching hospital, its data quality initiative, and its use of a variant of IP-Maps. These have been developed and used to model, analyze, and improve the quality of patient-level data that the hospital must submit to the Office of Statewide Health Planning and Development (OSHPD).

Case Study LTH Health System

The LTH Health System is made up of an 875-bed academic medical center plus affiliated physician groups, outpatient clinics, and the full range of postacute services, including skilled nursing beds, a rehabilitation unit, and a home health care agency. The medical center is one the largest nonprofit hospitals in the western United States, with an annual volume of about 50,000 in-patient admissions, including deliveries, and 150,000 out-patient and emergency room visits.

In this setting, as in most major hospital-centered health care delivery entities, the data derived from operational transaction systems (admissions, discharge, and transfer; medical records; patient billing; laboratory; pharmacy) feeds into strategic analyses and to external review agencies. This set of data was historically regarded as a by-product of providing care to patients and of secondary importance. Moreover, in many ways the "gold standard" means of data transmission in health care was essentially an illuminated manuscript in the form of the patient's medical record. Now, however, many strategically important initiatives, such as clinical quality and efficiency improvement, business development analyses, and required regulatory and government reports, are considered to be at risk because the data used to monitor and support these organization processes has been judged incorrect or incomplete or otherwise faulty to some degree.

Not only can the unacceptable levels of data quality compromise the ability of an organization to operate successfully in a competitive managed care environment, but it can also place it at risk of audit by external agencies such as the Office of the Inspector General and the Joint Commission on Accreditation of Healthcare Organizations. Recognizing that data is a valuable corporate asset, leadership at LTH concluded that the strategic use of data from diverse internal transaction system sources demands intelligent and disciplined management of data quality. Administrative leadership was successful in introducing and nurturing a customer-oriented accountability system with a focus on measurable continuous improvement over the last six to eight years. As a result, addressing these information quality issues was framed in this context, and information quality goals were included as part of the annual planning process beginning with the 1997–98 fiscal year.

Information Quality Context

Administrative leadership for the LTH information quality initiative was assigned to the Data Provider Group (DPG). This group was chartered as a multidepartmental working group by the CEO during the latter part of the 1996–97 fiscal year to address ongoing discrepancies observed in analyses produced by different departments using different databases that supposedly contained the same information. The DPG is chaired by the senior vice presidents of medical affairs and of finance. The membership includes the vice presidents of medical affairs, information systems, and finance as well as representatives from the departments of information systems, resource and outcomes management, health information/ medical records, patient accounting, cost accounting, budget, and reimbursement.

Since March 1997, in an effort to create a more customer-oriented and efficient information systems function, the senior vice president of medical affairs (to whom the vice president for information systems reports) has restructured that function and has communicated regularly with the management group about the changes. The changes included a new over-sight system for information systems governance made up of multi-departmental committees of information customers; a new systematic approach to evaluating all information systems acquisitions; the system-atic replacement of outdated hardware and software, including mak-ing PCs more widely available and establishing a common e-mail and calendar-scheduling system; the construction of an institutional intranet for the on-line distribution of various kinds of information; the construc-tion of a new ORACLE data warehouse; and the implementation of a new generic data query/report-writing tool for data analysis.

The development and implementation of a basic set of on-line manage-ment reports was established as a DPG goal for the 1997–98 period. The work plan adopted by the DPG included responsibilities for six subgroups, one of which focused specifically on data quality issues. The measure of success for the on-line management reports project was established as "an increase in the level of satisfaction with the manage-ment reports" throughout the health system. The DPG decided to adapt the IQA survey (see chapter 3) to measure this, and moved to establish a baseline assessment for all data users throughout the health system with the first administration of the modified IQA survey in December 1998. A follow-up was administered in May 1999.

Upon the completion of the on-line management reports project, the data quality subgroup was chartered by the DPG to continue its work more broadly and hence became the Data Quality Management Working Group (DQMWG), with a charge to establish a plan to systematically identify, monitor, and address data quality problems in order to assure that LTH data is "fit for use" for decision-making requirements. The DQMWG is made up of representatives from departments that are data collectors, data custodians, and data consumers (see table 10.1). Its basic functions are to establish ongoing measures of data quality that can be routinely updated and graphed for trends, and to establish routine pro-cesses to identify, track, and resolve data quality problems.

Thus the work described in this chapter occurred in an institutional con-text in which the need for active management of information products was recognized and in which administrative leadership had been estab-lished for that purpose. Although this work represents approximately two years of effort, it is only the starting point on a long journey.

Table 10.1
Data Quality Management Working Group Membership

Department/Area	Data Quality Roles
Resource and Outcomes Management	Chair, Consumer
Health Information	Collector, Consumer
Enterprise Information Systems	Custodian
Patient Financial Services	Collector
Cost Accounting	Collector, Consumer
Materials Management	Collector, Consumer
Operating Room Services	Collector, Consumer
Medical Network Services	Collector, Custodian, Consumer
Managed Care Contracting	Consumer
Pathology	Collector, Consumer

Patient-Level Data Submission

The state's Office of Statewide Health Planning and Development (OSHPD) requires every acute-care hospital to submit 31 data elements describing each patient discharge every six months (see table 10.2). The state establishes specifications for the quality of each of these required data elements and provides those specifications as public information. Data that does not meet the specifications is rejected, and the offending hospital is required to correct the data and resubmit it within a specific time frame.

In the recent past, changes in legislation have resulted in the imposition of a daily monetary fine for each day that a facility remains in noncompliance with established specifications beyond the deadlines for correction. Thus there are two types of immediate costs associated with poor-quality data submitted to OSHPD: the internal cost of the rework needed to make the required corrections, and externally imposed monetary fines. But there are additional costs as well, since these 31 data elements are at the heart of almost all internal efforts to analyze patient care for management and strategic purposes. These data quality problems could compromise institutional decision making based on such analyses.

Historically, LTH's data submissions to OSHPD always required corrections for one or more of the data elements, and the level of rework was not observed to diminish over time, suggesting that systematic improvements in the production of the data submission as an informa-

Table 10.2
OSHPD Data Elements

1. Patient's Type of Care	19. Principal Procedure Date
2. Hospital ID	20. Other Procedure Codes
3. Date of Birth	21. Other Procedure Dates
4. Sex	22. Principal E-Code
5. Race/Ethnicity	23. Other E-Codes
6. Race/Race	24. Patient's Social Security Number
7. Zip Code	25. Disposition of Patient
8. Admission Date	26. Total Charges
9. Source of Admission/Site	27. Abstract Record Number
10. Source of Admission/Licensure	(Optional)
11. Source of Admission/Route	28. DNR Order
12. Type of Admission	29. Expected Source of Payment/Payer
13. Discharge Date	Category
14. Principal Diagnosis	30. Expected Source of Payment/Type
15. Principal Diagnosis at Admission	of Coverage
16. Other Diagnoses	31. Expected Source of Payment/Plan
17. Other Diagnoses at Admission	Code Number
18. Principal Procedure Code	

tion product were not occurring despite the corrections of the immediate problems for each submission. It was estimated that at least 1,500–2,000 person-hours may have been required annually to make the needed corrections. In light of this continuing wasted effort in rework, made more onerous by the imposition of monetary fines by OSHPD, and with the establishment of the Data Quality Management Working Group as a viable entity, an effort was initiated to systematically evaluate and improve the quality of the data submitted to the state under this program. Thus the OSHPD Patient-Level Data Submission Improvement Project was set up.

Data Submission Improvement Project

The project was framed as a three-month effort to study how to improve the quality of the patient-level data submitted to OSHPD. LTH adapted the classical performance improvement approach, which was used for all its clinical and administrative performance improvement activities. The model is based upon the notion that all improvements are changes, but not all changes are improvements. In order to know whether a change is an improvement, three principles must be addressed: (1) a goal must be clearly articulated that unambiguously describes what is to be accomplished; (2) a measure must be established that objectively allows determination that the change has had an effect in the appropriate direction; and (3) a series of changes that are hypothesized to be improvements are tested and evaluated using Plan-Do-Study-Act (PDSA) cycles. Those changes that result in improvements are then implemented on an ongoing basis. In the early stages of a performance improvement project, the initial PDSA cycles focus on evaluating the work process to be improved.

A three-month project period was set from April through June 2000. The deliverables for the project were defined as (1) to prepare data production flow maps for all required data elements; (2) to identify where breakdowns occurred in the production process for each data element; and (3) to recommend improvements to prevent breakdowns from occurring in the future. It was felt that the benefits would go beyond the avoidance of monetary penalties and the elimination of costly rework needed to correct the errors, contributing as well to overall strategic decision making and compliance with other external oversight initiatives by the federal government and the independent Joint Commission on Accreditation of Healthcare Organizations. The project thus followed the classical performance improvement approach from an initial analytic phase in which the work process itself is defined and described, and viable measures for evaluating improvements are proposed, through to the point of producing a list of changes hypothesized to be improvements, which could then be tested following the project period and implemented if successful.

It was LTH's observation that attempts to "just fix" the data quality problems resulted in the rejection of its data submission by the state. The development of flow diagrams to describe the creation of the OSHPD submission data set as an information product would be a critical contribution to achieving lasting improvements in the quality of the data. It was apparent anecdotally that there were various causes of poor data quality in each information system involved, such as inaccurate data entry and unanticipated consequences of data transformations in interface programs, and these were multiplied by the number of information systems involved to create a truly complex environment in which no one participant could single-handedly resolve any particular data quality problem.

Gathering Background Information

The primary challenge of the project was to gather sufficient background information to unambiguously describe the information product supply chain from source to final output. This effort represented the first PDSA cycles of the improvement project, in which drafts of information product maps were produced and reviewed for revision and correction until a commonly accepted version was finally produced. The information was gathered through a series of open-ended background interviews with representatives of each of the departments involved. Prior to this project, there was no commonly accepted and unambiguously articulated vision of the overall work process that yielded this information product as its output. Instead, each of the several departments involved was able to articulate only its own role (although usually in an incomplete fashion), and each believed that errors were being introduced into the production process by other departments.

The 31 data elements required for submission to OSHPD were evaluated to identify the information system from which they originated. In some instances, data elements required for submission were not available in the required format from source systems, and those elements had to be constructed from other precursors that were available. In those cases, the precursor data elements were evaluated to identify their source systems. It was determined that all the required data elements originated in three source systems: the patient management system, the medical records system, and the patient accounting system. On this basis, representatives of the departments responsible for producing the required data elements were identified and interviewed to capture and record the unique knowledge each could contribute about how each data element was produced and managed in its source system, and about what were the issues of concern from each participant's point of view.

Through these interviews, additional information was also gathered regarding the intermediate transfer, processing, and storage of the data elements after they were extracted from the source systems and before they were consolidated into the final information product. Departments and individuals responsible for these intermediate steps in the information product supply chain were also identified and interviewed. In a similar fashion, information was gathered about and interviews were conducted with departments and individuals responsible for the final steps of data consolidation and the production of output files for submission. In some cases, the same departments and individuals were responsible for multiple steps in the production process, not necessarily sequentially. Multiple interviews were conducted with most department representatives in order to be certain that the information was being recorded correctly, and to answer additional questions that arose as more information was collected.

Finally, in addition to the describing the current process by which the OSHPD submission was produced, it was necessary to gather sufficient information that would allow LTH to assess the impact on the current process of new information system developments already under way. Two related developments were foreseen at that time that would have a big impact on this production process. First, within 18 months two of the three source systems currently used (the patient management system and the patient accounting system) would be replaced by a new combined information system currently in development. Second, the replacement of one of those systems, the patient accounting system, would result in the termination of the vendor relationship through which the submission to the state had historically been handled. This development would mean that LTH would have to begin to "cut the tape" for the submission itself, rather than simply managing a third party to accomplish this step of the production process.

During all these interviews, available background documentation was also identified and collected, whenever possible. This background documentation was analyzed as well, and used to confirm information gathered in the interviews. The background documentation consisted of data entry protocols for the three source systems, data definitions from OSHPD, edit criteria from OSHPD, tape layout parameters for the OSHPD submission, and the OSHPD rejection reports. The rejection reports were used to quantify and summarize the error history.

Developing Information Product Maps

Although LTH started by evaluating 31 required data elements, the hospital was able to describe the process by which the information product was assembled in terms of four basic information product maps (IP-Maps), one for each of the three source systems and one to describe the anticipated information systems transitions. Generally, these maps reflected a cross-functional approach and included a multilevel analysis of the data flow on the basis of department, physical location, information system, and business process. Three maps showed the flow of data elements as they originated in the source systems and moved through various interfaces, ultimately ending up in the submission data set on the required medium. The fourth map reflected a migration plan that would accommodate the anticipated information systems transitions.

Each map indicated "SMS Black Box" to represent the current process by which a third-party vendor (SMS) aggregated and submitted the required data on the required medium to OSHPD. The vendor's internal computing environment was complex, and LTH did not believe it was worth the time to study it in detail because the migration plan called for the elimination of the vendor altogether. For the purposes of creating the IP-Maps, as long as LTH knew what went into the "black box" and what came out of it, and whether the data quality problems were the hospital's or the vendor's, the "black box" indication would be sufficient.

Information Product Maps

The IP-Map in figure 10.1 shows the supply chain for the 12 required data elements originating in the Cascade medical records information system. It shows that all these data elements were derived from the patient's medical record, which went to the health information/medical records department (HID) when the patient was discharged from the hospital. The coders abstracted the data elements when they received the patient's medical record and entered them into the Cascade medical record information system. Through a daily upload this data was automatically sent to the "SMS Black Box," where it was used for transactional purposes and stored. Every six months these data elements were aggregated with the other required data elements and placed on a tape or cartridge for submission to OSHPD.

The IP-Map in figure 10.2 shows the supply chain for the 15 data elements originating in the PMOC patient management information system. Four of these data elements underwent simple or complex transformations in order to create other data elements required for submission. Fourteen of these data elements were entered by the admitting

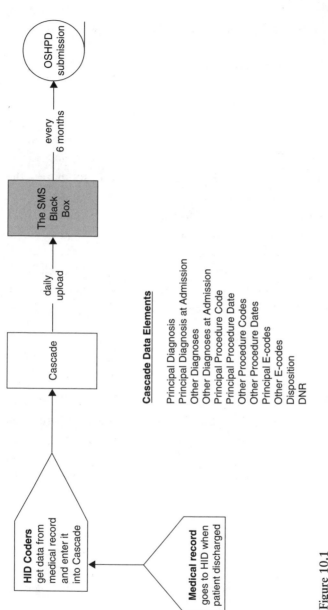

Figure 10.1
OSHPD Information Production Flow Detail: Cascade Data Elements

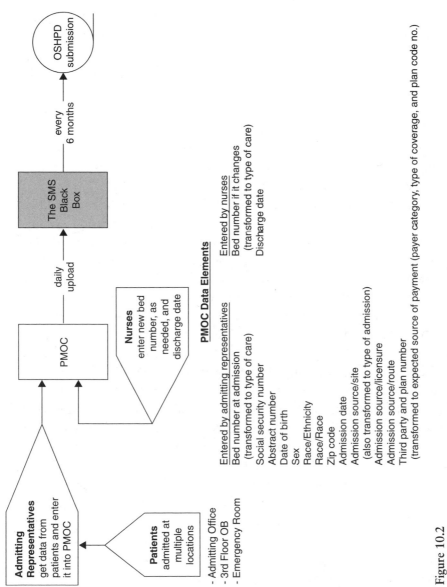

Figure 10.2
OSHPD Information Production Flow Detail: PMOC Data Elements

department by interviewing patients at the time of admission in a variety of locations. The admitting representatives got the data from the patients or their family members and entered it into the PMOC patient management information system. One data element (bed number) could be changed during the patient's stay by nurses. One data element (discharge date) was entered only by nurses. Through a daily upload this data was automatically sent to the SMS Black Box, where it was used for transactional purposes and stored. Every six months these data elements are aggregated with the other required data elements and placed on a tape or cartridge for submission to OSHPD.

The IP-Map in figure 10.3 shows the supply chain for the two data elements originating in the SMS patient accounting information system. One element, the hospital identification number, was hard-coded and never varied. The other, total charges, was aggregated from individual charges within the patient accounting system. The individual charges represented all the billable hospital services or supplies provided to the patient and were entered in the form of CDML (Charge Description Master List) codes by staff. There were three different methods of entering the codes. In some instances, CDML codes were entered directly into the SMS patient accounting system (within the "SMS Black Box"). In other instances, CDML codes were entered into the PMOC patient management system and automatically uploaded daily to the "SMS Black Box." Finally, some departments entered CDML codes into their own transactional systems (operating room, pharmacy, laboratory) which had their own upload schedules by which these codes were transferred to the "SMS Black Box." The individual charges were used for transactional purposes and stored. Every six months these data elements were aggregated with the other required data elements and placed on a tape or cartridge for submission to OSHPD.

The IP-Map in figure 10.4 shows the current flows and a migration plan that anticipates the new combined patient management/patient accounting system ("new PMOC") as well as the need for LTS to have an in-house data warehouse and produce the required output data for submission directly to OSHPD rather than through the SMS third-party vendor. On the original IP-Map, solid arrows show the three anticipated transition phases were distinguished by color-coding and differentiating lines. In figure 10.4, solid arrows show the current status of the flows

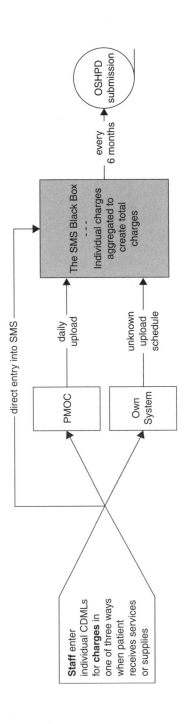

Figure 10.3
OSHPD Information Production Flow Detail: SMS Data Elements

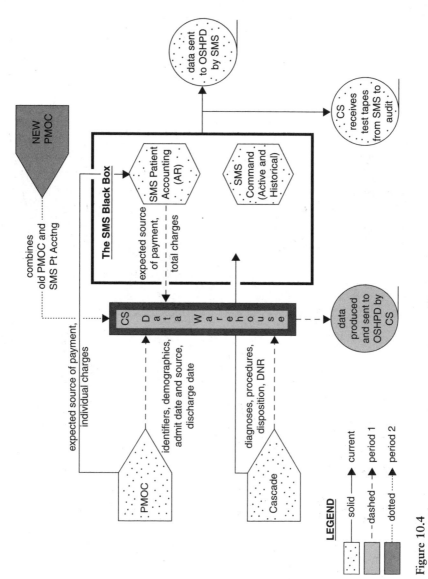

Figure 10.4
OSHPD Information Production Flow Overview: OSHPD Patient-Level Data Elements

and dashed arrows show the interim plan for the period until implementation of the "new PMOC." Dotted arrows indicate the final implementation of the "new PMOC." Some details are shown within the "SMS Black Box" to illustrate the interim plan for data capture.

In the interim plan, the information flow was modified so that all required data elements from the three existing source systems could be captured in the data warehouse and LTH could produce the required output data in-house and submit it to OSHPD in proper form. In the final implementation the "new PMOC" was to replace the former patient management and patient accounting information systems, and the combined data elements were to be sent by "new PMOC" to the data warehouse. The Cascade medical records system continued to feed data elements into the data warehouse.

Improvements Initiated: Current Process and Future Plan

As a direct result of LTH's efforts to develop the information product maps, the hospital was able to initiate specific and systematic improvements in the production process for the OSHPD submission data set and plan for future improvements as well. First, LTH obtained the audit criteria handbook and the audit program source codes in COBOL from the state and used these to develop audit programs in SAS for key problematic data elements. It then ordered a test tape from the vendor in advance of the required submission date so that it could audit the data set prior to submitting it to the state. The results of the audit were shared with the appropriate "owner" departments, and they were able to make some timely corrections in order to reduce the number of data quality problems identified by the state. While this may seem like an obvious strategy, it had never before been done.

LTH was also able to identify several constructed data elements to be modified to simplify the transformations required to produce certain OSHPD-required data elements from the data elements available in the source systems. In addition, LTH was able to offer useful suggestions to the team that was building the new combined patient management/patient accounting information system, in order to ensure that all OSHPD requirements would be built into this new system, both for data entry standards and routine audit procedures.

In the six months after the conclusion of the initial improvement project, LTH continued to initiate improvement cycles to advance its abilities to manage this information product more effectively. All these advances were based on the information product maps, which provided a common understanding of the complex processes involved and a common language with which to discuss them. LTH proactively managed each OSHPD submission, and although new unanticipated issues continued to arise, the hospital was much more confident in its ability to understand and address them. LTH initiated a pilot project to develop its capability for in-house production of the submission data set after discontinuation of the third-party vendor. Finally, as the new information system evolved, it was reconceptualized to include the medical record system and to reconfigure the old data warehouse as a more complete enterprisewide database. The Data Quality Management Working Group reconceptualized the information systems to ensure that the OSHPD-required data set could be produced in-house in an efficient and timely fashion, reducing to a minimum the need to integrate data from multiple sources or to transform data elements. The hospital was optimistic that this cumulated knowledge and experience could be studied, disseminated, and applied as a model for other LTH data quality improvement initiatives.

Concluding Remarks

It is instructive to review the LTH case and the optimistic projections with the benefit of hindsight. Some objectives were achieved, but others encountered unforeseen obstacles that prevented achievement or necessitated the reformulation of objectives. We describe here how the outputs of the improvement project were utilized and how they contributed to LTH's reaching various milestones in its journey along the road to data quality.

As intended, LTH was successful in its approach to finding and fixing the errors in its data prior to OSHPD submission. Also as intended, LTH's data submissions were accepted by OSHPD starting with the first official submission after completion of the project. In addition, each successful six-month submission was made prior to the due date. In this respect, the improvement project helped LTH achieve its fundamental objectives—to meet the state's accuracy, completeness, and timeliness requirements.

However, the broader objective of providing input to the team that was building the new combined patient management/patient accounting information/medical record coding system encountered many obstacles along the way. The importance of this broader objective should not be underestimated because it alone would enable LTH to prevent the creation of new errors.

Unfortunately, the new information system still has not been implemented. Its development has been fraught with much more difficulty than originally anticipated, and its implementation has been repeatedly rescheduled. Its development crises have resulted in erratic revisions to specifications and have been accompanied by regular staff turnover. As a result, motivating the actual incorporation of input related to designing the new information system to prevent the creation of errors turned out to require constant vigilance and continued advocacy.

This new information system is targeted to become the single source for all the OSHPD-required data elements, allowing the hospital to exercise complete control over every aspect of producing the submission data set. This is in contrast to the previous environment, in which the use of many proprietary vendor-driven applications as well as archaic and poorly documented programming code underlying home-grown systems and interfaces prevented the exercise of any control over most upstream sources of errors. Although LTH has not yet been successful in ensuring that its input will be fully utilized by the development team for the new information system, its ability to recognize these shortcomings and to plan explicitly to avoid them does represent another successful use of the output of the improvement project. LTH is thus able to illustrate a variety of methods by which the new system could help to prevent the creation of errors, and simultaneously support more efficient business processes.

First, the new information system can help eliminate the need for wasteful rework by allowing LTH to specify the data elements to be collected and their permissible values, besides populating them. By specifying as acceptable values for the OSHPD-required data elements only those values that require no transformation prior to submission, errors at present introduced into these transformations could be eliminated.

However, other competing interests may prevent this (such as UB-92 billing value requirements for the same data elements), so the new information system also gives LTH the capability of directly performing any transformations that might be needed.

In addition, built-in data quality management capabilities such as routine audit and feedback of discrepant or incomplete data values for real-time correction by upstream staff responsible for data creation could be included. This would reduce the creation of unacceptable data values at the source and thus prevent the population of downstream repositories with erroneous or incomplete data. Since the new information system will be one unified system, it also eliminates the need for programmed interfaces to move data from various source systems into a single staging repository prior to making it available for submission or retrospective analysis. It therefore eliminates the potential for inadvertent transformation of data as an unintended effect of programming approaches or errors in programming interfaces. Each of these methods can clearly help prevent the creation of the errors that LTH now finds and fixes, and in the aggregate have the potential to bring profound benefits to the institution through the elimination of wasteful rework.

Table 10.3
JCAHO Standards Related to Information Management Planning

IM.1	The hospital plans and designs information management processes to meet internal and external information needs.
IM.2	Confidentiality, security, and integrity of data and information are maintained.
IM.2.1	Records and information are protected against loss, destruction, tampering, and unauthorized access or use.
IM.3	Uniform data definitions and data capture methods are used whenever possible.
IM.4	The necessary expertise and tools are available for the analysis and transformation of data into information.
IM.5	Transmission of data and information is timely and accurate.
IM.5.1	The format and methods for disseminating data and information are standardized, whenever possible.
IM.6	Adequate integration and interpretation capabilities are provided.

Finally, from the broadest possible perspective, the improvement project did provide an example that has been emulated for several additional performance improvement efforts focused on other information management activities. The development of flow charts to illuminate several other intractable information management tasks has been most useful. Ultimately, this work has helped LTH better meet many of the hospital accreditation standards in the management of information to which the medical center is held accountable by the Joint Commission on Accreditation of Healthcare Organizations (JCAHO).

A close reading of the management of information standards shows that JCAHO intends that hospitals engage in explicit information management planning and performance improvement activities such as those described here. Listed in table 10.3 are the specific management of information (IM) standards that apply to information management planning activities.

Although LTH has not yet achieved all its goals, it did achieve its immediate objectives and has been able to use what it learned to help guide the organization in its journey to data quality. LTH has encountered unexpected obstacles along the way, and the lessons learned have been effective in helping LTH to address these obstacles constructively so that the journey can be continued. The experiences of LTH are a reminder that management strategies as well as technical solutions can have a profound impact on eventual success.

The benefits of incorporating the lessons learned seem obvious to LTH, but it is important to emphasize that it is not enough to advocate vigorously for a logical argument at a single point in time. The factors that influence attention and priorities at every level of the organization are varied and shifting, so the approach to data quality must accommodate to the specific environment. With LTH's tool kit of techniques and the accumulation of examples from which to learn, the hospital is confident that it can eventually learn how to overcome all obstacles on this journey and achieve all the benefits that high-quality data can provide to the organization.

11

Data Quality Policy

A clear statement of policy, disseminated throughout the organization, must be in place for a company to remain engaged and to succeed in maintaining a viable, continuing data quality effort, which in turn proactively supports business activities. A clearly articulated policy and specific, detailed prescriptions form the basis for any successful ongoing data quality effort. The data quality policy reflects the vision of the organization.

The preceding chapters have addressed a wide range of issues that must be faced and tasks that must be undertaken by any organization with the intention of seriously and proactively pursuing the goal of attaining and maintaining high-quality information and data. We have provided a perspective with which to approach the journey to data quality. We have described specific methodologies, tools, and techniques with which the organization can assess and improve its data quality. Where possible, we have included real-world examples to empirically demonstrate and supplement the conceptual materials. All these initiatives will be of no avail if the organization does not articulate and promulgate a clear data quality policy.

Many organizations have started the journey but have not been able to sustain the effort and keep the data quality activities going. Too often the activities are executed by a single champion or a single department that recognizes the benefits that can be obtained from such activities. The result is that the process is not institutionalized, and inertia within the rest of the organization leads either to a slow decay or an abrupt halt to all data quality initiatives. We firmly believe that a key to success in the data quality journey is the creation of appropriate organization policies that involve all functions and activities related to the maintenance of the data product.

A complete policy has different levels of details ranging from broad guidelines and principles to more detailed elaboration and specification of these principles. It addresses both data quality practice, such as management issues, implementation, and operational issues, and standards, and the quality of the data product itself.

In this chapter we provide ten broad policy guidelines that should form the basis of any organizational data quality policy. For each, we discuss subordinate principles and how these guidelines might be operationalized. Note that each organization should make sure that the resulting policies, practices, and principles are appropriate to the environment of the organization and take into account the history and culture of that organization.

Ten Policy Guidelines

In developing a data quality policy specific to an organization, an overarching objective is to put in place a policy that will lead to the continual improvement of the overall quality of the data for use. The questions that must be addressed are many. In what areas is improvement most important? Clearly, some of these areas will be business areas and business processes; others will be in the information technology itself. Some of the existing organization policies may have to be changed to ensure that the firm produces and uses data of high quality. The firm should also establish measures to gauge the effectiveness of the policy.

Who establishes the policy is also critical. The provenance of data quality policy should be the business side, not the information technology side, of the firm. There is no question that information technology departments are concerned about such matters as procedures for backup and recovery and establishing audit trails for changes. But a broader business perspective must be represented when establishing data quality policy for the organization.

The different roles required in managing information must be clearly identified, the responsibilities associated with each position must be clearly specified, and the interrelationships among the various roles must be clear. With respect to the data itself, it is imperative that data elements critical to the organization be identified and that all business functions within the organization share an understanding of the meaning and values that are used to represent the real world.

The ten policy guidelines that are proposed as the basis of an organization's data quality policy are distilled from our observation of the data quality practices of early adopters and of the evolutionary paths of the root conditions of data quality problems.

1. The organization adopts the basic principle of treating information as product, not by-product.
2. The organization establishes and keeps data quality as a part of the business agenda.
3. The organization ensures that the data quality policy and procedures are aligned with its business strategy, business policy, and business processes.
4. The organization establishes, clearly defined data quality roles and responsibilities as part of its organization structure.
5. The organization ensures that the data architecture is aligned with its enterprise architecture.
6. The organization takes a proactive approach in managing changing data needs.
7. The organization has practical data standards in place.
8. The organization plans for and implements pragmatic methods to identify and solve data quality problems, and has in place a means to periodically review its data quality and data quality environment.
9. The organization fosters an environment conducive to learning and innovating with respect to data quality activities.
10. The organization establishes a mechanism to resolve disputes and conflicts among different stakeholders.

1.   Treat information as product not by-product.

Treating information as product, not by-product, is the overarching principle that informs the other guidelines. This principle must be continually communicated throughout the organization. It must be a part of the organization's ethos. Without adherence to this principle, we believe that any data quality initiative will not yield long-term, measurable benefits.

2.   Establish and maintain data quality as a part of the business agenda.

An effective policy requires that the organization maintain data quality as part of the business agenda. The organization must understand and document the role of data in its business strategy and operations. This requires recognition of the data needed by the firm's business functions to complete their operational, tactical, and strategic tasks. It should be clearly understood that this data is fundamental to the competitive position of the firm. Sole responsibility for the formulation of data quality policy should not be relegated to the information technology function.

The responsibility for ensuring that data quality is an integral part of the business agenda falls on senior executives. Senior executives should understand their leadership is critical to success and that they must be proactive in fulfilling the leadership role. They must take an active part in ensuring data quality in the organization.

Improving data quality can lead to the identification of potential areas of improvement in business processes or to the uncovering of previously unrecognized critical business processes. Because such occurrences can have a marked impact on the competitive position of the firm, senior management must be proactively involved in the data quality effort. Maintaining data quality as part of the business agenda implies that the data is recognized and treated as an integral component of the business. This is a given in today's data-intensive economy. Among the activities to achieve this integration the organization should identify and define the data needed to perform its business activities. Further, it must actively manage its data quality practices. Of importance is the establishment of key data quality performance indicators. These must be identified, measured, and adjusted when conditions warrant. The feedback from these indicators can result in business processes' being modified.

3.   Ensure that data quality policy and procedures are aligned with business strategy, business policy, and business processes.

The primary function of data is to support the business. To do so, the data quality policy must be in place and consistent with the organization's business policy. This implies that a broad view of what constitutes data policy is necessary. An integrated, cross-functional viewpoint is a prerequisite to achieving an aligned data quality policy. To achieve proper alignment requires high-level executive involvement. It is likely that without senior management's active involvement, misalignment will occur and data quality problems will manifest themselves. Proper alignment will also foster the seamless institutionalization of data quality policy and procedures into the fabric of the organization's processes.

Improper alignment or too narrow a focus can cause data quality problems and prove disruptive to the organization. It can lead to conflict that could have been avoided. For example, a view that restricts data quality policy to technical details of data storage and ignores the uses of the data at different levels of decision making would result in misalignment and subsequent problems.

In short, data quality policy should reflect and support business policy. It should not be independent or isolated from business activities.

4. Establish clearly defined data quality roles and responsibilities as part of organization structure.

Clear roles and responsibilities for data quality must be established. There should be specific data quality positions within the organization, not ad hoc assignments to functional areas in times of crisis. Additionally, one of the fundamental goals data quality function should be to identify the data collectors, data custodians, and data consumers, and to make members of the organization aware of which of these roles that they and others play.

Roles and responsibilities specific to the data quality function range from the senior executive level to the analyst and programmer level. Current examples of titles from practice include Chief Data Officer, Senior VP of Information Quality, Data Quality Manager, and Data Quality Analyst.

In appendix 1 of this chapter we provide example job descriptions of different data quality positions. These descriptions are extracts from actual job descriptions used by a large organization. Each organization should develop descriptions specific to its needs and environment.

5. Ensure that the data architecture is aligned with the enterprise architecture.

The organization should develop an overall data architecture that is aligned with and supports the enterprise architecture. By enterprise architecture we mean the blueprint of the organizationwide information and work infrastructure. The data architecture helps promote a view of the information product that is consistent across the enterprise. This promotes shareability of information across the organization.

The data architecture reflects how the organization defines each data item, how data items are related, and how the organization represents this data in its systems. It also establishes rules and constraints for populating each data item. All of these are essential elements of any product— a definition of the item, statements indicating how it is related to other entities in the business, and what constraints exist for populating it in various databases.

To ensure that the data architecture is aligned and remains aligned with the enterprise architecture entails a number of specific and detailed tasks. For example, establishing a data repository is critical to the development and maintenance of a viable data architecture. The organization should generate a set of metadata that clearly define the data elements and provide a common understanding of the data. This allows for efficient data sharing across the organization. It is always wise to follow widely accepted data management practices.

Appendix 2 of this chapter provides a set of data architecture policies used in a global manufacturing company.

6.   Be proactive in managing changing data needs.
The data needs of consumers change over time. We use the term *consumers* to mean any individuals or enterprises internal or external to the organization who use the data of the organization. If there is one constant that data consumers face, it is that the environment in which they operate will always be changing. This is also a constant for the organization.

An organization has two choices: either react promptly to these changes in the environment or face a loss of competitive advantage, market share, and customer loyalty. To maintain a high degree of data quality, the organization must be sensitive to changing environments and changing needs. This entails continual scanning of the external environment and markets and of the changing needs of internal data consumers.

It is also critical to the maintenance of high data quality that the rationale for changes in policy and procedures be clearly and promptly communicated throughout the organization. Steering committees and forums can play a crucial role in the dissemination of this information.

We add a caveat at this point. The organization must remain cognizant of local variances as they relate to global data needs. In today's multinational and global firms, long-standing local culture and customs exist. These local differences must be clearly identified and policy adapted to incorporate those local variances that make sense.

7. Have practical data standards in place.

It is easy to get people to agree that standards should be in place. It is much more difficult to reach agreement on what should be standardized and the prescription of the standard. At times, it is difficult to obtain agreement on the definitions of the most basic data elements. Data standards entail many areas of data practice. Addressing the following questions will help inform the process of instituting practical data standards. Should the organization use external standards or develop standards internally? If external standards are to be used, which ones should be chosen? Does the standard apply locally or globally? In either case, how and when will it be deployed? What processes are appropriate to monitor and adopt changing standards over time? How should they be documented and communicated?

The process that an organization uses to determine whether to choose external or internal standards, and under what conditions, should be developed. The preferred solution would be to use a standard that has been created and maintained by an organization other than the organization using the standard. If this is possible and acceptable, then which existing standards to adopt must be determined. This may be a choice between international, national, or industry standards or between two national standards. For example, the International Standards Organization (ISO) has a standard set of country codes. One's first choice would be to choose the international standard. Other things being equal, this provides the greatest degree of flexibility and lowest costs to the firm.

If no external standards are available, the organization will have to establish its own set of standards. These should adhere to good data quality practices. Once established, the standards should be easily accessible and broadly communicated to the organization.

Not all standards will be implemented on an enterprisewide basis. Some standards may apply to only one business function in one geographic area. These boundaries must be clearly established. It is also possible that an enterprise standard cannot be realistically or practically instituted throughout every part of the organization concurrently. In this case, the timing of adoption in different parts of the organization must be incorporated into the implementation plan. If required, a plan for implementing across geographic areas should be developed. Policy should explicitly state that lessons learned in deploying standards in one part of the organization be captured and disseminated when deploying the standards in other units of the organization.

Policies should be developed to manage changing standards over time. This requires specifying who is responsible for monitoring and initiating changes. Typically, the consumers of specific data would be scanning the environment for changes in standards. The unit responsible for periodic reviews of data standards should be alerted and, if appropriate, should initiate changes in standards. It is critical that when standards are changed, policies and procedures be in place to communicate the changes to the organization.

8. Plan for and implement pragmatic methods to identify and solve data quality problems, and have in place a means to periodically review data quality practice and the data product.

Pragmatic methods based on the diagnostic methods and measures described earlier should be promoted as standard methods across the organization. These techniques can be adapted and applied by different units to develop local variants that are consistent with the organization at large. The diagnostic methods and auditing techniques described in chapters 4, 5 and 6, if used consistently, will provide historical time lines of the data quality and help to identify existing and potential problems.

As is true for any working system, be it a transportation system, a social system, or an information system, it is standard practice to periodically audit the system to ensure that it is in working order and fulfilling its objectives. Periodic reviews are a must for data quality practice and programs. As we pointed out earlier, it is all to easy to allow a data quality program to lapse and to lose any progress made.

To help avoid this pitfall, periodic reviews of the data quality environment and the overall data quality of the organization is a must. One method to achieve this is to assess the data quality practice and the firm's data quality using a standard assessment survey. Multiple assessments over time using the standard survey provide a series of assessments against which the firm can measure its progress. Further, if an evaluation of an exemplar organization is available, the firm can use this exemplar's results as a benchmark and evaluate its performance against this benchmark.

We have developed such an instrument, the Data Quality Practice & Product Assessment Instrument (see appendix 3 of this chapter). The instrument assesses the organization along lines that correspond to the guidelines specified in this chapter. The first part evaluates the data quality practice of the organization, which includes executive management and implementation and operations issues. The second part evaluates the data product, which includes control of the data as well as the degree of the data's fitness for use. This instrument has been used quite effectively, for example, in a major U.S. teaching hospital. Note that the specific items listed in the instrument can also be used to generate specific tasks.

A practice related to the auditing task involves certification of data. Data of both transaction systems and data warehouses must be included in the certification process. A robust process of data certification will ensure that data practice and data product will be of high quality. As a consequence, a data certification policy must be put in place. The policy should stipulate that sources for the information be clearly identified, including definitions, valid values, and any special considerations about the data. If the organization is gathering data in a new way, and reports already exist that represent some aggregation including this data, it is imperative that one can either demonstrate exactly the same reporting results or document clearly why the differences exist. It is especially important to identify and document why differences exist to avoid having the credibility or believability of the data questioned. As part of the data certification policy and process, procedures dealing with actions to be taken when data quality issues arise must be established.

When first implementing a certification process, it is important to understand the difficulties that users of existing reports might have if it is determined that the existing reports have to be changed or will change as higher-quality data is used to prepare the reports. For instance, if sales aggregations change because there is better control and classification of the source data, many users of the reports may lose comfort with the new reports and will vigorously challenge them. One should not underestimate the difficulty of the certification process.

9. Foster an environment conducive to learning and innovating with respect to data quality activities.

Initiatives that contribute to a learning culture would include the use of a high-level data quality steering committee, the installation of forums across the organization, and the stress on continuous education and training. All should be strongly supported by senior management.

Other steps can be taken to cultivate a learning culture. The organization should put in place a policy of rewards, and if necessary, sanctions, that are consistent with achieving a high level of data quality and maintaining this high level. What should not be discouraged is the identification and reporting of data quality problems, even if these prove embarrassing to management. Nipping a problem in the bud will prove much less embarrassing than allowing a problem to fester and grow into a major source of irritation to internal users and external customers. Employees should feel free and safe to report data quality problems openly. A formal mechanism for reporting such problems can help in this regard. Establishing a forum for data collectors, data custodians, and data consumers to voice and share data quality problems and discuss data quality issues will be of great value. This will also aid in the dissemination of the experiences of the collectors, custodians, and consumers and foster an appreciation of each other's perspectives and roles.

Communication mechanisms can be used to communicate data quality successes and promulgate good solutions. These lines of communication can also be used to share difficult problems and disseminate up-to-date industry benchmarks, new research findings, and the like. Employees directly involved with the data quality program should be encouraged, to participate in data quality conferences, workshops, and industry forums. In short, the organization must remain engaged. These initiatives should foster a continuing learning culture.

As part of a viable learning environment, the organization should use data quality improvement experiences across industries as benchmarks and learning experiences. As data quality initiatives grow within an industry and across industries, new benchmarks, best practices, and success stories will be available. These should be used by the organization as markers against which its performance can be compared and its processes improved. First adopters will serve as benchmarks for others. This can redound to the first adopter's benefit in that by sharing its experience with other, less advanced organizations, problems not yet encountered may surface. This will be important feedback to the first adopter in that it may prompt analysis of unforeseen future problems.

As part of any process that is meant to increase the overall data quality within an organization, it is necessary to construct education and training programs appropriate for each of the major roles we have identified that are involved in the data quality process: data collector, data custodian, and data consumer. To enhance the results of the process and to make sure that the data requirements of the business are followed, training programs tailored for each role must be developed. Each role should have training that addresses core data principles and data quality policies. In addition, an organization should provide specific training that is applicable to each role. Much has been written about the training for data custodians, who usually reside within traditional information technology departments. Specific attention should be paid to making sure that data collectors and data consumers understand the critical roles that they play within the overall data quality environment. The training must be given to all stakeholders in the enterprise.

It is especially important for data collectors to understand why and how consumers use the data. Data collectors also must adhere to the data quality principles as they enter the data even though they are not the prime beneficiaries of such activity and they do not usually get measured on this portion of the data entry task. Data consumers are critical to providing appropriate feedback on the quality of the data they receive, including whether it is needed data. This function would include apprising the data collector of changes in data needs. Data custodians must recognize that although they are not directly responsible for the data, they must understand its purpose and use. As with data collectors, data custodians should be aware of how and why data consumers use the data.

The importance of data quality policies, good data practices and principles, effective data quality training, and communication within the organization cannot be overemphasized. This often overlooked portion of data quality practice can mean the difference between those that are successful in this journey and those that are not.

10.   Establish a mechanism to resolve disputes and conflicts among different stakeholders.

Data policy disputes, jurisdictional disputes, data definition disagreements, and data use debates will occur. The organization must have in place a mechanism or a set of related mechanisms to resolve these differences and any conflicts that may result. These could be a set of hierarchically related mechanisms corresponding to different levels of the firm. Their form is not as important as their existence and that they have a clear charter specifying their responsibilities and authority.

Any of a number of conflict resolution techniques and mechanisms can be used. The specifics must be consistent with an organization's business strategy and culture. Examples are use of steering committees, data quality boards, data quality work groups, or data quality councils. The scope of responsibility, the degree of authority, and clearly defined lines of reporting and communications must be specified. Ambiguity in the specifications will render these resolution mechanisms ineffective.

It is most important that a historical record be maintained of the disputes and their resolutions. This institutional memory will serve the organization well as it adapts to changing future environments.

Concluding Remarks

We presented a set of ten policy guidelines that an organization can use to develop a solid data quality policy. Each organization will adapt these principles to fit its environment. However the guidelines are implemented, the basic intent behind them should remain clear: to provide the vision and guidance for a sustainable, viable, and effective data quality practice. If this is accomplished, the organization will be able to confront future data quality challenges and adapt to a changing environment. The principles, concepts, and techniques needed to provide high-quality information in the organization will have been institutionalized and data of high quality ensured.

Appendix 1: Job Descriptions of Data Quality Positions

Example Job 1. Senior Analyst, Data Quality Management

Position Summary   This position supports the department's data/information quality management effort. This is accomplished through the application of data quality management principles and practices in cross-functional teams that aim to improve data integrity and information usability in the various data systems. Works with the Data Quality Management Manager, business data owners, data warehouse staff, and data users to develop and implement data quality standards and practices across the institution. In carrying out these duties, the Data Quality Management Senior Analyst provides analytic and change process support to various data content creation departments, such as Admissions, Hospital Operations, and Health Information (Medical Records). Under direction of the Data Quality Manager, this position will also take the lead on developing and producing the Data Quality Dashboard to consist of objective and subjective measures of data and information quality, to support data quality improvement initiatives. Subjective measures will be derived from the Information Needs and Information Quality Survey, which this position will be responsible for fielding on an annual basis, analyzing the results, and preparing graphs and tables for presentation. In addition, this position will be responsible for researching and developing data production maps or flow charts for specified data elements or information products, and for drafting data quality policies and procedures for inclusion in the Policies and Procedures Manual. This position will work in a collaborative fashion with the Programmer for Data Quality Management and all other members of this department and other departments across the Health System, as required.

Educational Requirements

• Bachelor's degree and extensive course work in a quantitative field is required. Some course work or background in statistics is preferred.

• Master's degree in appropriate field (such as Public Health, Hospital Administration, Health care Informatics, Biostatistics Health System) is preferred.

Experience

• Minimum of three years' experience in the acute care setting functioning in the role of a data analyst.

• Experience in facilitating peformance improvement projects is preferred.

• Demonstrated understanding of data/information quality principles and practices.

• Knowledge of business intelligence tools such as Crystal, Brio, Business Objects, and Cognos is desirable.

• Strong problem-solving skills and persistence to solve difficult problems.

• Must possess solid verbal and written communication skills for working effectively on cross-functional teams.

Example Job 2. Data Quality Health System Manager

Position Summary   The goal of the data quality management function is to assure that usable data is available for analysis, reporting, and operations as well as strategic decision making. This position will recognize and promote the importance of data and information as valuable resources. The Health System Manager will lead the Data Quality Management unit to set policies and plans for the definition, organization, protection, and efficient utilization of data. The position will promote the management and coordination of the creation, use, storage, documentation, and disposition of data. The primary purpose of this position is to promote information quality through data consistency and standardization. This may be achieved by developing standards for data element names, definitions, values, formats, metadata, and documentation in a central data repository and in databases. This position is also responsible to provide in-depth consultation in the areas of design, modeling, and content of data retrieval, storage, and analysis. This requires an in-depth understanding of the organizationwide data systems, analysis tools, data needs, and the data itself. This also requires a broad knowledge of quality improvement and clinical outcomes, and now they are related to the data. Knowledge and experience in the area of clinical care enhance this position. Works independently in a coordinated fashion with all department staff; establishes and maintains effective liaison with all appropriate departments and divisions; develops and maintains a positive work environment.

Educational Requirements   Demonstrated expertise in operational problem solving, performance improvement, systems analysis, and statistical analysis, as acquired through completion of at least a Master's degree in health care administration or business or related field.

Experience

• Minimum of 5 years' experience in a health care organization or a consulting organization providing services to the health care industry, or equivalent combination of education and work experience.

• Advanced computer skills, including knowledge of computer applications to perform database management, spreadsheet analysis, statistical functions, word processing, presentations, and project management, and the ability to understand the larger scope of companywide information systems. Skilled in working with relational databases. Working knowledge of health care data types and in-depth understanding of the meaning of this data.

• Demonstrated ability to organize and analyze large volumes of information. Excellent organizational skills; ability to prioritize work effectively. Self-motivated and able to manage multiple tasks simultaneously.

• Excellent written and verbal communication skills. Ability to work collaboratively in order to gain cooperation, facilitate change, and influence decisions with all levels of management, employees, and supervisors of other hospital departments on a continual basis.

• Must be able to work as part of a team.

• Ability to facilitate discussions, teach, and train concepts related to data retrieval, data analysis, data integrity, and analytical information systems.

Physical Requirements   Normal physical requirements for administrative responsibilities carried out at a desk, ability to walk to and from meetings among the buildings on campus.

Work Environment   Prolonged use of computer keyboard and CRT; routine office environment with prolonged sitting.

Example Job 3. Data Quality Management Programmer

Position Summary   This position supports the department's data/information quality management effort. This is accomplished through the application of data quality management principles and practices in cross-functional teams that aim to improve data integrity and information usability in the various data systems. Works with the Data Quality Manager, business data owners, data warehouse staff, and data users to develop and implement data quality standards and practices across the institution. In carrying out these duties, the Data Quality Management Programmer provides ad hoc and routine programming and analytic support evaluating databases, data repositories, and reporting routines emanating from those sources along a variety of data quality dimensions, making use of data production control procedures and practices. Under direction of the Data Quality Manager, this position takes the lead on developing and maintaining the data quality issue/adverse event database. This position works collaboratively with the Senior Analyst for Data Quality Management and all other members of this department and other departments across the Health System, as required.

Educational Requirements

• Bachelor's degree and extensive course work in computer programming is required.
• Some course work or background in statistics is preferred.

Experience

• Minimum of three years' SAS programming experience. Skills in various modules such as Basic, Statistics, and Graph.
• Programming experience within acute care setting with knowledge of health care adminstrative, financial, and coding data.
• Trained in relational database, such as Oracle, PL/SQL, and SQL.
• Experience in developing and maintaining databases in Oracle, SAS, or Access.
• Demonstrated understanding in data/information quality principles and practices.
• Knowledge of business intelligence tools such as Crystal, Brio, Business Objects, and Cognos is desirable.

• Strong problem-solving skills and persistence to solve difficult problems.
• Must possess solid verbal and written communication skills for working effectively on cross-functional teams.

Example Job 4. Medical Staff Information Supervisor

Position Summary   This position supervises the integrity of the medical staff information chain, starting from its source in the originating application through any programmed interfaces or extracts and including any downstream databases, files, tables, or applications from which analyses or reports are derived that make use of any of the data elements originating from the source.

This position's primary internal customers are the management and staff of the Medical Staff Services department. In addition, other internal customers include all other departments and staff that enter data into the originating application, including but not limited to the departments of Graduate Medical Education, Continuing Medical Education, and Health Information (Medical Records Chart Completion), as well as departments and staff that rely on using that data for their day-to-day patient care work, including but not limited to Nursing, Admissions, Operating Room Services, and Health Information (Medical Records Coding). In addition, the position serves as the primary liaison with all appropriate information technology units to ensure effective management and maintenance of application, database, and Web servers from both hardware and software perspectives.

At this time, the Medical Center utilizes the MSO application to originate the medical staff information chain and as the "gold standard" source for all data collected by the Medical Staff Services department to support the medical staff application and credentialing process and subsequent granting of privileges to members of the medical staff for admitting patients and performing various clinical procedures. It is expected that the incumbent will become the in-house expert for this application, learning and supervising all aspects of data entry as well as all query and reporting capabilities, and teaching other users on an as-needed basis to ensure that this information system is fully supporting the Medical Center's business processes relative to its relationship with its medical staff. In the future, should the Medical Center decide to discontinue the use of the current application and initiate use of an alternative application to meet this need, the incumbent would continue to carry out a similar set of responsibilities utilizing the alternative application as well as play a key role in the transition to the alternative.

In carrying out these responsibilities, this position leads working teams as needed (including department-specific and interdepartmental teams) to ensure integrity of medical staff information anywhere in the institution; develops and maintains knowledge of all applications, databases, interfaces, and extracts that contain or include medical staff data; and supervises the resolution of any data quality problems or issues as well as efforts required to prevent future data quality problems or issues.

Educational Requirements

• Bachelor's degree and extensive course work in quantitative field is required.
• Course work or background in computer science or statistics is preferred.
• Master's degree in appropriate field is desirable.

Experience

• Advanced computer skills, including knowledge of analytic query, reporting, and relational database management tools (e.g., Access, Brio, Crystal, SQL, Oracle), spreadsheet analysis, statistical functions, word processing, presentation development, project management, e-mail, browsers, and on-line reporting.
• The ability to understand the larger scope of companywide information systems.
• Experience with networking operations and Web-based information dissemination tools is helpful.
• Working knowledge of HTML and Microsoft FrontPage.
• Strong familiarity with software testing, interface testing, and validation of results.
• At least five years' related work experience in an acute hospital care setting, or an equivalent combination of education and work experience.
• Proven track record of providing leadership, innovation, and vision for health care professionals working with computerized information systems.

• Ability to work in teams, ability to lead teams; ability to work independently; ability to effectively supervise the working of non-direct-report staff to achieve project objectives.

• Excellent verbal and written communication and presentation skills with both technical and nontechnical personnel as well as quantitative analysis skills are required.

• Ability to structure and manage multiple projects and tasks in a fast-paced, dynamic, and complex environment. Flexibility to accommodate unstructured situations and changing priorities.

Appendix 2: Data Architecture Policy Example from a Global Manufacturing Company

Data is treated as an integral component of the business.

• Business identifies the information needed to perform its activities.
• Business is involved in the active management of data quality processes.
• Data management is treated as a focused discipline with dedicated personnel.
• Ownership of data is clearly defined (responsibility, accountability, and empowerment).
• Concern for data quality ranges from the individual field through the downstream enterprise systems that use and rely on the data.
• Consumers of data are considered customers.

Key performance indicators are established for data quality.

• Measure and provide incentives against key performance indicators.
• Adjust other processes.

In-stream data quality checks are performed on data and its associated processes.

• Data entry processes have non-negotiable checks and balances built into their daily flow to ensure that sound data management practices are followed.
• Validation process checks are executed to ensure accuracy, completeness, and uniqueness.
• Second-level reviews are conducted for critical data.
• Sign-off is required for extremely critical data changes.
• Audit trails of data changes are created and reviewed.

Poststream data quality checks are performed on data and its associated processes.

- Conduct cyclical system-level and enterprise-level audits.
- Actively interrogate data, looking for potential defects and anomalies.
- Cross-check data for inaccurate data, incomplete data, and obsolete data.
- Cross-check data for heterogeneous duplicates (records that represent the same item but are entered into the system in a way that results in bypass of the system's duplication edits).
- Ensure that related data is kept in synch.

Root analysis is conducted for defects uncovered.

- Review defects, looking for patterns of problems.
- Trace data problems back to the point of origin.
- Look for associated data errors that may not have surfaced yet.
- Document the analysis with suggested preventive measures.

Risk analysis is conducted periodically for the pitfalls of defective data.

- Analyze existing data, assessing the potential impact of bad data and the likelihood of its occurrence.
- Analyze potential changes to data or processes, and identify any new or altered risks that may result.
- Document the analysis, and suggest process changes to mitigate the risks.

Appendix 3: Data Quality Practice & Product Assessment Instrument

Data Quality Practice & Product
Assessment Instrument

Copy # _____   **Participant Name:** _____

Instructions: In the comments, please write as much as is needed. The cell will expand automatically.

Assessment Score Scale: 1 means poor and 7 means excellent.

DQ Criteria	score (1 to 7)	Comments
Part 1: Data Quality Practice		
I. Management		
A. Involvement of executive level of the organization		
(1) Highest executive levels of the organization appreciate and understand the crucial role that DQ plays in the organization and in the organization's strategic goals		
(2) Executives at the highest level of the organization establish and foster DQ as part of the business agenda		
(3) Major DQ initiatives are championed at the highest executive level and are driven from these top levels		

DQ Criteria	score (1 to 7)	Comments
B. Policy and management procedures in place		
(1) Enterprise-wide policies are in place to define roles and responsibilities for managing organizational data		
(2) Enterprise-wide mechanisms and structures in place that assign responsibility and accountability for organizational data		
(3) Enterprise data needs are developed and communicated based on business strategy		
(4) Data quality functions are promulgated at enterprise-wide level and the awareness and understanding of data quality practice are fostered		
(5) Formal review panel and procedures to adjudicate disputes and disagreements on data requirements among different stakeholders are in place		
(6) Formal procedures to arbitrate differences among stakeholders regarding data standards and definitions are in place		
(7) Clear policy on rewards and sanctions with respect to the value of data quality work is developed and enforced		
(8) A formal record of violations and enforcement actions is kept and knowledge derived from these actions is promulgated		

DQ Criteria	score (1 to 7)	Comments
C. The organization takes a proactive approach in managing changing data/information needs		
(1) Policy and procedures are in place to monitor and establish changing business needs at all levels of the organization		
(2) Cross-functional, formal review panel and documented procedures are in place to manage configuration control, that is, changes to data models, data standards, and data elements in response to changing business needs and changing organizational goals		
D. The organization internally fosters a learning environment with respect to DQ/IQ		
(1) The organization develops and supports forums to discuss organizational data quality as an ongoing practice		
(2) Clearly stated policy of training in data quality practice is in place		
(3) A clearly identified person or group is responsible for supporting end-users questions about data uses		
II. Implementation and Operations		
A. Data architecture is aligned with business processes		
(1) Data architecture is documented and promulgated throughout the organization		

DQ Criteria	score (1 to 7)	Comments
(2) Data architecture is published for easy access and understanding by people who use the data		
(3) Data architecture captures appropriate enterprise entities and attributes		
(4) Formal procedures and policies in place for updating the data architecture and for promulgating the update		
(5) Person/group accountable for data architecture in place		
(6) Formal review procedures instituted to periodically and proactively review data architecture		
(7) Formal procedures for approving, disseminating, and implementing changes to data architecture are in place		
(8) Formal mechanism in place to monitor and enforce data architecture		
B. Source data are properly validated		
(1) Procedures to validate source data are documented and implemented		
(2) Source data documentation is required and available		
(3) Random audits of source data are conducted		

DQ Criteria	score (1 to 7)	Comments
(4) A formal record of violations and enforcement actions is kept and knowledge derived from these actions is promulgated		
(5) Data sent out from source systems are certified by responsible source to be of high quality		
C. Audits are systematically conducted to monitor all phases of DQ		
(1) A group responsible for audits and for disseminating information on audits exists and functions actively		
(2) Random audits of source data feeds are conducted, defects documented, and information disseminated to affected stakeholders		
(3) Random audits of stored data are conducted, defects documented, and information disseminated to affected stakeholders		
(4) Random audits of data delivered to end-users (consumer data) are conducted, defects documented, and information disseminated to affected stakeholders		
D. Effective configuration control policies, procedures, and processes for changes to data standards and data are in place and enforced		
(1) Procedures and approval authority signoffs on changes and updates are documented and implemented		

DQ Criteria	score (1 to 7)	Comments
(2) Changes to data standards and formats are approved and communicated to all stakeholders		
(3) Formal procedures are in place to control changes to data standards and definitions		
(4) Formal procedures are in place to manage data updates		
E. Control and management of sharable data		
(1) Documented policies and procedures that define what data is sharable and how sharable data is provided to a new user are in place		
(2) A list of the users of sharable data and the data they use is maintained and promulgated throughout the organization		
(3) Formal procedures are in place to notify users (of shared data) that data will be updated prior to updates		
(4) Changes in sharable data are communicated throughout the organization in timely fashion		
F. Data tool kit is current, appropirate, and actively managed		
(1) A formal evaluation process to determine best DQ tools that meet requirements is in place		

DQ Criteria	score (1 to 7)	Comments
(2) Formal procedures and suitable test sets to evaluate effectiveness of DQ tools are in place		
(3) Appropriate Cleansing/Profiling/Auditing tools are used where appropriate		
(4) Appropriate ETL tools are used where appropriate		
(5) Data production maps that trace data flow from source to data consumers have been created		
G. Data Knowledge and Data Skills are integral part of orrganizational knowledge		
(1) Relevant personnel at all levels of the organization have a good understanding of DQ principles and methodologies		
(2) Organization promotes attendance at data quality classes/seminars		
(3) Personnel are given exposure to leading DQ projects and to DQ industry practices		
(4) Organization follows appropriate methods for recording and sharing organizational knowledge on data quality		
(5) Data production maps are developed, maintained, and used		

DQ Criteria	score (1 to 7)	Comments
Part 2: Data Product		
A. Extent to which metadata are complete and maintained		
(1) Meaningful enterprise-wide metadata standards exist at database-level		
(2) Meaningful enterprise-wide metadata standards exist at data element level		
(3) Meaningful enterprise-wide metadata standards exist at data-value level		
(4) Metadata is up to date at all three data levels		
(5) Procedures to update and maintain metadata are documented and implemented		
B. Degree of control of source data		
(1) Degree to which business rules related to source data are documented and implemented		
(2) Degree to which source data are certified to authenticate the data before transmission		
(3) Degree to which source data embody data consumers requirements		
(4) Degree to which source data are prepared in line with the capacity and technology of data storage facility		

DQ Criteria	score (1 to 7)	Comments
C. Degree of compliance to data integrity constraints in stored data		
(1) Formal process to review definitions for data integrity and to enforce the constraints are in place		
(2) Domain integrity rules are adhered to		
(3) Column integrity rules are adhered to		
(4) Entity integrity rules are adhered to		
(5) Referential integrity rules are adhered to		
(6) User-defined integrity rules are adhered to		
D. Degree to which data are usable, that is, fit for use by the data consumer		
(1) Data are easily and quickly retrievable for access		
(2) The volume of data is appropriate for the task at hand		
(3) Data are regarded as credible and believable		
(4) Data are not missing and are of sufficient breadth and depth for the task at hand		
(5) Data are concisely represented		
(6) Data are presented in a consistent format		

DQ Criteria	score (1 to 7)	Comments
(7) Data are easy to manipulate and apply to different tasks		
(8) Data are correct and free of error		
(9) Data are in appropriate languages, symbols, and units, and the definitions are clear for interpretation		
(10) Data are unbiased and objective		
(11) Data are applicable and relevant to the task at hand		
(12) Data are highly regarded and reputable in terms of their source or content		
(13) Access to data is restricted appropriately to maintain its security		
(14) Data are sufficiently up-to-date for the task at hand		
(15) Data are easily understandable		
(16) Data are beneficial and add value to a task from their use		

12
End of the Journey?

The environment in which an organization operates will change. New opportunities will present themselves. New problems will arise. From these types of events, new data needs will arise. New and improved techniques and approaches will be explored and developed. A viable and vibrant data quality program should be capable of adapting to and accommodating the changing environment. A viable data quality program will require constant vigilance. Complacency is always around the corner. The journey never ends.

It is fitting to end this book by briefly addressing the problems of data quality that will confront organizations in the future and introducing research ideas and innovative applications that will be part of the continuing journey to data quality. Many of these initiatives build on the ideas and techniques discussed in the previous chapters of this book.

Recapitulation

We promoted the view that information should be treated as product, not by-product, as a fundamental principle of any data quality initiative. We made the case for continually promoting awareness of data quality throughout the organization and for institutionalizing data quality in the organization. Early on, we stressed the need to make the economic case for a data quality program and presented ways of so doing. The importance of clearly articulating the value proposition for data quality cannot be overemphasized.

We discussed a number of methodologies, tools, and techniques with which to achieve awareness and develop a data quality program. A basic diagnostic methodology that rests on both qualitative and quantitative evaluations of the organization's quality of data was introduced. Of note is the idea that the subjective evaluations must be obtained from the different stakeholders in the process, the 3Cs—the collector, the custodian, and the consumer of data.

Given that the task of examining every item in the data pool is prohibitive from both a time and cost basis, we introduced some basic techniques to statistically sample databases to assess quality of the data.

We explicitly addressed the problem of root causes and the techniques of root cause analysis. How these root conditions can be manifested, both in positive and negative ways, was presented. Intervention strategies to address these problems were introduced. We presented both short-term interventions and the longer-term interventions, which are the preferable ones to employ.

We introduced the constructs associated with information product maps. Work continues to refine the constructs of IP-Maps and their application.

We ended with the suggestion of ten guidelines that the organization can use to articulate a comprehensive data quality policy. Without a coherent, cohesive, and comprehensive data quality policy, the organization will find it difficult to sustain an ongoing data quality program.

We introduced, where possible, reality in the form of case examples from existing organizations. These can be used to validate our prescriptions. More important, however, they can serve as guides and benchmarks for the organization that is beginning the journey to data quality. Some of the techniques presented in this book are already in the repertoire of analysts, and we have simply applied the constructs to data quality. Other constructs and techniques along with the tools such as IP-Maps, the IQA survey, the Integrity Analyzer, and the Data Quality Practice & Product Assessment Instrument are specific to problems in data quality and represent the latest (but not final) state of the art.

Where does the field go from here? What new challenges have emerged? What additional new techniques are on the horizon? How will the journey continue? It is appropriate to end this book by briefly examining these issues.

Future Challenges and General Concerns

It has been said that "the only constant is change." This is both true and false in regard to the journey to data quality. It is true in that the environment changes, posing new problems; research continues and new knowledge and techniques are developed. It is false in that after years of identifying problems and developing solutions, the same problems resurface in new or changing environments. History repeats itself as newer organizations repeat the mistakes of their predecessors and organizations that have succeeded in improving their data quality suffer relapses or fall into the trap of thinking that once data quality problems are solved their work is finished.

What are the data quality challenges that organizations continue to confront? The problems are both old and new. By old we mean the standard problems associated with the basic evaluative data quality dimensions. These will always be of concern and must be attended to. The ongoing struggle to ensure that the data are free of error, are timely and useful, will continue. These problems, however, will manifest themselves in new ways and in new situations as business processes change, as they become more complex, as the volume of data continues to expand, and as data is put to more and more uses.

A challenge that is increasingly prominent is that of data integration. Appropriate integration of data across multiple sources and multiple feeds presents formidable quality problems. Here the challenge is twofold: how to achieve the appropriate integration and, at the same time, maintain the different users' views of the same data. It also raises the important and challenging issues of security, confidentiality, and changing degrees of sensitivity.

Customer relationship management (CRM), supply chain management (SCM), business risk management (BRM), business intelligence (BI), and other business practices have allowed organizations to make significant progress in understanding and managing corporate data and relationships. However, because of the complexity and speed of change in today's business environment, better knowledge of the data is needed. In this regard, the general challenges of corporate householding surface (Madnick, Wang, and Xian 2004; Madnick et al. 2005).

Knowledge about organizations and their relationships is known as corporate household knowledge, and the process of obtaining and managing corporate household knowledge is known as corporate house-holding.

The practice of data quality both impacts and can be impacted by data mining. Data-mining techniques, in particular, data exploration tech-niques, can be applied to aid in the discovery of poor quality data and data problems. From the application viewpoint, the impact of poor data quality on the models of data mining is also well documented, and a great deal of effort is invested in cleansing and preparing data before it is mined (Han and Kamber 2001).

An important challenge facing data quality analysts is that of rating the quality of data with respect to its fitness for use. One of the basic tenets expounded in this book is that data of good quality is data that is fit for use. The specification of fitness for use will vary depending on how, what, where, why, and when the data is used. Developing tech-niques that include this type of knowledge in the data requires continued research.

Last, a major problem area that must be addressed in data quality practice is security. The general area of security presents multiple prob-lems. We must be concerned with the sensitivity level of the data, ensur-ing that it is not accessible to everyone, but rather on a need-to-know basis. Organizations face the requirement of maintaining confidentiality of the data. This responsibility accrues partly from the organization's re-lationship with and obligations to its customers. It also is legally man-dated by federal and state governments.

All these challenges are exacerbated by the continued advance and adoption of wired and wireless technology.

The challenges we have listed are not exhaustive, but they serve to cre-ate the context within which one can view some of the current research approaches and techniques. We do not present these as finished prod-ucts. Rather, they indicate the directions that the research is taking. If, however, the constructs presented in this chapter inspire students and practitioners of data quality to modify, adapt, extend, and adopt the concepts and techniques or to develop their own unique approaches, this chapter will have served its purpose.

Formally Capturing the Quality Characteristics of Data

The quality characteristics of data must be available for the analyst to make a judgment as to whether the data is fit for use. None of the hierarchical, network, or relational data models were developed with data quality in mind. Although the relational model includes data integrity and normalization, these capabilities are not useful in determining whether the data stored in the underlying relational database is timely, accurate, or credible. New approaches must be developed to explicitly accommodate data quality characteristics. Renewed attention to this area is necessary. Some initial research that addresses this problem is the work on attribute-based data quality DBMS (Wang, Reddy, and Kon 1995) and on a quality entity relationships (QER) model (Storey and Wang 1998).

Attribute-Based Data Quality DBMS

In essence, the attribute-based data quality DBMS model facilitates cell-level tagging of data. The model defines an extended version of the relational model by defining a set of quality integrity rules and a quality indicator algebra. These rules and indicators allow one to process SQL queries that have been augmented with quality indicator requirements. From these quality indicators, the user can make a better interpretation of the data and determine the believability of the data.

Zero defect data may be neither attainable nor necessary. It would be helpful when using the data to have knowledge of, or to able to judge the quality of, the data. For example, in making a financial decision to purchase stocks, it would be important to know who originated the data, when and how the data was collected, and what its deficiencies might be.

The basic approach is to apply Codd's idea of a tuple ID, a system-wide unique identifier of tuples. An attribute in a relational scheme is expanded into an ordered pair, called a quality attribute. This pair consists of the attribute and a quality key. The model refers to the expanded scheme as a quality scheme. Correspondingly, each cell in a relational tuple is expanded into an ordered pair, called a quality cell, consisting of an attribute value and a quality key value. This expanded tuple is referred to as a quality tuple, and the resulting relation is referred to as a quality relation. Each quality key value in a quality cell refers to the set of quality indicator values immediately associated with the attribute value. This set of quality indicator values is grouped together to form a quality tuple called a quality indicator tuple. A quality relation composed of a set of these time-varying quality indicator tuples is called a quality indicator relation. The quality scheme that defines the quality indicator relation is referred to as the quality indicator scheme.

The quality key concept enables one to link an attribute with its quality indicators and to link a quality indicator to the set of quality indicators with which it is associated. The algebraic development of the model is beyond the scope of this book, but details can be found in Wang, Reddy, and Kon (1995) and Wang, Ziad, and Lee (2001).

Quality Entity Relationships Model

Before one can implement the cell tagging required by the attribute-based data quality DBMS model, the relevant data quality characteristics must be specified. Ideally, these should be identified, specified, and incorporated at the conceptual design stage of a database application. Storey and Wang (1998) have suggested a quality entity relationship model that is an extension of Chen's (1976) entity relationships model, a methodology that is used extensively in database design.

The traditional entity relationships model has evolved to capture entities, relationships, attributes, and other advanced constructs such as "is-a" and "component-of" relationships. Specific information on data quality is not explicitly captured. Any incorporation of data quality is left to the individual designer. The need for a formal system, an algebra or calculus to define and manipulate such data descriptions has long been recognized.

As noted, Storey and Wang suggested an extension to the basic entity relationships model, the QER model, intended for such a use. They gave a detailed quality database design example illustrating the logical design and the corresponding relational database development (see table 12.1). The context is that of the design of a course database. We note that this work is far from complete in terms of a formal, closed, and complete design method. Much additional development needs to be done. Nevertheless, the concepts and constructs can be of use as they stand.

Table 12.1
Conceptual Design for the Course Database

Step 1. *Identify user requirements.*
What courses are available, their certification data and cost? What classes are offered for a course?
Who is the instructor of a class?
Accuracy and timeliness measures of class attendance, description of what the measures mean
(Data quality requirements)
What standards are required for a course and a course's rating?
(Application quality requirements)

Step 2. *Identify application entities.*
Course (name, base cost, recertification period, description)
Class (name, attendance, actual cost)
Instructor (name, phone no.)

Step 3. *Identify application quality entities.*
Standard (name, description)
Standard rating (name, value, interpretation)

Step 4. *Identify data quality entities.*
Dimension (name, rating)
Measure (description, rating)

Step 5. *Associate application entities with application quality entities.*
Course–Standard (course name, standard name)

Step 6. *Associate application entities with data quality entities.*
Class Attendance–Dimension (class name, dimension name)

Step 7. *List the application relationships.*
Course has Class(es)
Instructor teaches Class(es)

Step 8. *List the application quality relationships.*
Course has Standards
Course Standard has Standard Rating

Step 9. *List the data quality relationships.*
Class Attendance has Data Quality Dimension
Class Attendance–Data Quality Dimension has Measure

Corporate Householding

Much of the material in this section is borrowed directly, with permission, from the seminal papers on corporate householding (Madnick, Wang, and Xian 2004; Madnick et al. 2005).

Context plays a large role in how entities should be known and understood. A customer, typically a corporation, can be viewed in multiple ways from within the same organization depending on context. Units within a corporation have different relationships, perspectives, and concerns related to a customer (or supplier, partner, competitor). A few examples of these perspectives and concerns include financial credit risk, products and markets in marketing area, and legal liability.

These perspectives represent different views of the customer. The number of points of contact between two corporations can easily reach into the hundreds or thousands. To be of use to business, corporate household information needs to be understood and organized in a clear and meaningful way.

Knowledge about organizations and their internal and external relationships is known as corporate household knowledge. The process of capturing, analyzing, understanding, defining, managing, and effectively using corporate household knowledge is known as corporate householding.

Corporate householding provides a way to identify, understand, organize, and use certain types of information and knowledge in a manner that allows the corporation to strategically harness this knowledge and to answer critical business questions. This knowledge includes the following:

• Knowledge of corporate relationships and potential relationships and structures, such as

a. Structures within the corporation, e.g., departments, divisions, subsidiaries, branches;

b. Structures represented by organizational charts;

c. Relationships with business customers, partners, suppliers, competitors;

d. Relationships with third-party intermediaries such as dealers, distributors, brokers, agents, and resellers;

e. Relationships with governing and regulatory bodies.

• Knowledge of how, where, when, and why these relationships operate.

• Knowledge of all the ways in which a corporation conducts business with related organizations and knowledge of business relationships between that organization and its related entities such as intermediaries, that is, transparency of relationships so that the corporation can "see" all its indirect relationships.

Three common but major problems that corporate householding must address are

• When are two things the same? (Entity identification)
• When to include whom or what? (Entity aggregation)
• Is it necessary to know and, if so, do we know who are the suppliers of our suppliers? (Transparency)

Entity Identification

Problems can arise from the sometimes ambiguous naming of a particular entity, for example, IBM. Many names can refer to exactly the same entity (International Business Machines Corporation, IBM, IBM Corp., IBM Corporation). In other words, one entity can appear to be multiple entities, making it difficult to identify an entity correctly and efficiently. This kind of challenge is known as entity identification.

Entity Aggregation

Even after we have determined that "IBM," "International Business Machines," and "Computing-Tabulating-Recording Co" all refer to the same entity, we need to determine what exactly that entity is. That is, depending on the context, what other unique entities, such as Lotus Development Corporation, should be included or aggregated into the definition of "IBM."

Consider another example. The MIT Lincoln Lab is "the Federally Funded Research and Development Center of the Massachusetts Institute of Technology." It is physically separated from the main campus of MIT. Problems arise when trying to answer business questions such as, "How much was MIT's budget last year?" and "How much did we sell to MIT this year?" Should the Lincoln Lab employees, budget, or sales be included in "MIT" calculations, and in which cases should they not be?

Answers to such questions will differ depending on the context in which they are asked. Under some circumstances, Lincoln Lab should be included in "MIT," whereas in other circumstances it should not be. This type of challenge is referred to as entity aggregation.

Transparency

Relationships between entities often have complex multilayers. For example, MIT purchases computers from IBM both directly and through local computer stores (e.g., CompuUSA). In this case, MIT buys from CompuUSA, but CompuUSA's supplier is in fact IBM. This is the classic case where a seller sells its products both directly and through a broker.

So what is the answer to the question "How much did MIT buy from IBM last year?" Are only direct purchases to be counted, or should indirect ones be included also? This particular example predates IBM's sale of its PC business to Lenovo.

Whether an organization is interested in the interface between the seller and the broker or the one between the seller and the ultimate buyer (via the broker) also depends upon the context—different answers will be appropriate for different circumstances. Knowing when these interfaces are important, and how to capture and organize knowledge about them, is a challenge known as transparency.

Current research in corporate householding addresses such issues.

Data Mining

Data quality plays an important and direct role in the area of data mining. Data mining techniques can be applied in the search for poor quality data. Alternatively, the quality of the data is always of concern when data mining is used as part of the business intelligence effort.

Standard data exploration techniques can be applied to discover deficiency in a data set. Indeed, we introduced this notion earlier in this book. We did not refer to it as data mining, however. Nevertheless, some of the techniques described in previous chapters, including the use of the Integrity Analyzer (CRG 1997b), can be considered rudimentary data explorations for poor quality. Examples include counting the frequency of missing values in a column or counting the number of violations of referential integrity.

A generic data-mining technique widely used in marketing or market basket analysis, association rules, may also prove useful in exploratory analysis for poor data quality. Although not envisioned for this purpose, the use of algorithms that generate association rules may provide insight into relationships in the data which are suspect or erroneous.

From the model builder's perspective, the quality of the data used can significantly affect the results of data-mining algorithms and the models generated in data mining. Indeed, a great deal of effort is placed in cleansing and preparing the data for use by data-mining algorithms. Typically, three types of dirty data confront the analyst: missing data, noisy data, and inconsistent data. The processes used to cleanse such dirty data are detailed in many data-mining books (e.g., Berry and Linoff 2004).

Taking a more expansive view, the final objective of data mining is to produce results (data) in response to either specific or generic questions regarding a specific data set and the hidden information this data set may contain. In short, the intent is to produce results (data) that are fit for use. A key point is that one must ask the appropriate question; otherwise the results may be valid but not fit for use. The output may meet several major quality characteristics of data (e.g., complete, free of error, consistent) but may not be fit for use (no value added) because the initial question was inappropriate.

Assuming that the question is appropriate, other points of concern are easily identified. Clearly, the source data can be dirty. If it is not cleansed, the results may be highly distorted or unusable. The cleansing process is intended to prepare the data for mining. This process, however, can also lead to problems if the data is improperly cleansed or excessively modified to create a data set suitable for the data-mining technique to be used. Choice of the data-mining technique can also contribute to poor results (poor quality, unfit for use). This will occur if the wrong technique is applied to answer the question. Of all the possible events, this should be the least likely to occur because of the extensive experience with data-mining algorithms in the field.

Once the data is cleansed, a number of different techniques, appropriate to different problem types, can be applied to perform the mining. These techniques include neural network representation, supervised and unsupervised models, logistic regression, induction of decision trees using, for example, Quinlan's C5.0 algorithm, association rules analysis using, for example, the a priori algorithm, and a number of clustering approaches. Details of these approaches can be found in Berry and Linoff (2004), Han and Kamber (2001), and Hand, Mannila, and Smyth (2001).

We offer an additional, somewhat unorthodox view of the relationship between data quality and data mining. To date, it has received little, if any, attention. Specifically, included in our broad view of high-quality data is that data be usable and that it add value. In this sense, data that has been mined and that has yielded additional information because of the mining initiative is data whose quality has been enhanced by the data-mining process. To put it another way, if data yields useful business intelligence and information previously not known, its quality has been enhanced.

Prior to being mined a pool of data may have potential for wider use than originally intended. We call this its latent potential. As more knowledge from the data is gained, new uses may emerge. Data mining can help achieve this condition and discover this previously latent potential. Some preliminary work, which it is hoped will lead to linking the cost of data cleansing and the results of different mining techniques, has been reported (Pipino and Kopcso 2004). Regardless of perspective, data mining and data quality are inextricably linked, and further research will add to the knowledge and tool boxes of the data quality analyst.

Data Integration

A challenge that is increasingly prominent is that of data integration. Appropriate integration of data across multiple sources and multiple feeds presents formidable quality problems. Here the challenge is twofold: how to achieve the appropriate integration and at the same time provide specific views of the same data for different data consumers. Several issues beyond technical data integration are involved in this quest. Consider the continuing debate and discussion on appropriate solution directions such as standardization versus the evolutionary approach.

For example, context interchange (Madnick 1999) is a nonintrusive approach for data integration that keeps the autonomy of local data collection, storage, and use intact. The basic tenet is to translate the intended meaning of data between the receiving and the sending sides. Long-held and assumed local use and customs, such as the way people use calendar units and monetary units, are typical examples. Semantics and rules are easily translated. The more serious and difficult question involves understanding the original or several sources of data when the data travels among several systems, organizations, and countries without explicit trace or tag attached to it. The contexts of data are often lost when it is moved from the original system or place.

Security

A major problem area that must be addressed in data quality practice is security. We must be concerned with the sensitivity level of the data, ensuring that both the technical and nontechnical aspects, such as security policy and training, are managed properly. Organizations face the requirement of maintaining confidentiality of the data. This responsibility accrues mainly from the organization's relationship with and obligations to its customers. It also is legally mandated by federal and state governments. As such, the security and confidentiality issues are always discussed along with accessibility. Clearly, organizations need to proactively identify the issues, have an opportunity to formulate resolutions, and communicate the resolution and the direction using their explicit data quality policy.

A broader issue is that of national security. This has increasingly become the central issue in the United States and other countries. When information needed to make a timely decision that impacts national security is pulled from diverse sources, the quality of the source information used and the integration techniques and processes applied are of critical importance to a country and its populace.

These security issues become more complicated and challenging as we move to a globally connected world. We turn our attention to this challenging area, that of the globally wired and wireless world.

The Wired and Wireless World

This rapidly emerging and rapidly changing communication environment poses potentially complex data quality challenges to organizations. It also supports our contention that the journey never ends. The data quality challenge has evolved from a single medium (text-based systems) to multimedia. The challenge has also evolved from one of relatively uncomplicated sources and processes to complicated and unknown sources of data.

In this globally distributed, rich data environment, it becomes increasingly difficult to distinguish between the provider/collector, the custodian, and the consumer. Additionally, we do not know how many iterations or cycles through different information production systems have occurred. How many sets of three Cs have been involved and have acted on the data? Increasingly, tracing data to the original source becomes difficult.

In such an open environment, transformation of data occurs without disciplined documentation. Some information on the context from which the data emanated and in which it exists may be lost. Information that keeps track of these cycles would help. It is clear that the problems an organization will have to confront are truly intimidating. On the other hand, organizations and data quality professionals will have great opportunities to engage in producing innovative solutions proactively.

The basic principles and policies covered in this book will still hold. The implementation of these principles and policies will take on different forms and will require adaptation and innovation.

A Final Observation

New problems, old problems not completely solved, new technologies and techniques, all will provide new and exciting challenges (Lee 2004). Some will be anticipated and some will be totally unexpected.

Some organizations have already begun to address the newer challenges. The three real companies represented by our vignettes in this book are examples. They have embarked on advanced phases of the journey. They have begun to promote data quality practice outside their organizations, sharing their insights and experiences, and they have initiated training programs within and external to their organizations.

Armed with the principles and techniques discussed in this book, with new advances that are on the horizon, and, most important, with the hard-earned experiences accrued during the initial phases of the data quality journey, seasoned organizations will be well prepared to continue the journey and help others begin the journey.

References

Agmon, N., and N. Ahituv. 1987. "Assessing Data Reliability in an Information Systems." *Journal of Management Information Systems* 4 (2): 34–44.

Amram, M., and N. Kulatilaka. 1998. *Real Options: Managing Strategic Investment in an Uncertain World*. Boston: Harvard Business School Press.

Anthes, G. 2002. "Bridging Data Islands." *Computerworld* (October 14): 23–24.

Argyris, C., and D. Schön. 1978. *Organizational Learning: A Theory of Action Perspective*. Reading, Mass.: Addison-Wesley.

Arnold, S. 1992. "Information Manufacturing: The Road to Database Quality." *Database* 15 (5): 32.

Ballou, D., and H. Pazer. 1985. "Modeling Data and Process Quality in Multi-input, Multi-output Information Systems." *Management Science* 31 (2): 150–162.

Ballou, D., and H. Pazer. 1995. "Designing Information Systems to Optimize the Accuracy-Timeliness Trade-off." *Information Systems Research* 6 (1): 51–72.

Ballou, D., and H. Pazer. 2003. "Modeling Completeness versus Consistency Trade-offs in Information Decision Contexts." *IEEE Transactions on Knowledge and Data Engineering* 15 (1): 240–243.

Ballou, D., and G. Tayi. 1989. "Methodology for Allocating Resources for Data Quality Enhancement." *Communications of the ACM* 32 (3): 320–329.

Ballou, D., and G. Tayi. 1999. "Enhancing Data Quality in Data Warehouse Environment." *Communications of the ACM* 42 (1): 73–78.

Ballou, D., R. Wang, H. Pazer, and G. Tayi. 1998. "Modeling Information Manufacturing Systems to Determine Information Product Quality." *Management Science* 44 (4): 462–484.

Bardhan, I., S. Bagchi., and R. Sougstad. 2004. "Prioritizing a Portfolio of Information Technology Investment Projects." *Journal of Management Information Systems* 21 (2): 33–60.

Batini, C., M. Lenzirini., and S. Navathe. 1986. "A Comparative Analysis of Methodologies for Database Schema Integration." *ACM Computing Survey* 18 (4): 323–364.

Becker, S. 1998. "A Practical Perspective on Data Quality Issues." *Journal of Database Management* 35 (Winter): 35–37.

Berry, M., and G. Linoff. 2004. *Data Mining Techniques for Marketing, Sales, and Customer Relationship Management.* 2d ed. Indianapolis: Wiley.

Black, F., and M. Scholes. 1973. "The Pricing of Options and Corporate Liabilities." *Journal of Political Economy* 81 (3): 637–654.

Bobrowski, M., and S. Vazquez-Soler. 2004. "DQ Options: Evaluating Data Quality Projects Using Real Options." In *International Conference on Information Quality*, 297–310, Cambridge, Mass: MITIQ.

Bovee, M., B. Mak, and R. Srivastava. 2001. "A Conceptual Framework and Belief Function Approach to Assessing Overall Information Quality." In *International Conference on Information Quality*, 311–328. Cambridge, Mass.: MITIQ.

Brackett, M. 2000. *Data Resource Quality Turning Bad Habits into Good Practices.* Upper Saddle River, N.J.: Addison-Wesley.

Brackstone, G. 1999. "Managing Data Quality in a Statistical Agency." *Survey Methodology* 25 (2) (December): 139–149.

Brodie, M. 1980. "Data Quality in Information Systems." *Information and Management* (3): 245–258.

Cappiello, C., C. Francalanci, and B. Pernici. 2002. "A Model of Data Currency in Multi-Channel Financial Architectures." In *International Conference on Information Quality*, 106–118. Cambridge, Mass.: MITIQ.

Cappiello, C., C. Francalanci, and B. Pernici. 2003–2004. "Time-Related Factors of Data Quality in Multi-channel Information Systems." *Journal of Management Information Systems* 12 (3) (Winter): 71–92.

Carey, R., and R. Lloyd. 1995. *Measuring Quality Improvement in Healthcare: A Guide to Statistical Process Control Applications.* New York: ASQ Quality Press.

Celko, J., and J. McDonald. 1995. "Don't Warehouse Dirty Data." *Datamation* (October 15).

Chen, P. 1976. "The Entity-Relationship Model: Toward a Unified View of Data." *ACM Transactions on Database Systems* (1): 166–193.

Chen, Z. 2001. *Data Mining and Uncertain Reasoning.* New York: Wiley.

Chengalur-Smith, I., D. Ballou, and H. Pazer. 1999. "The Impact of Data Quality Information on Decision Making: An Exploratory Analysis." *IEEE Transactions on Knowledge and Data Engineering* 11 (6): 853–864.

Chisholm, M. 2001. *Managing Reference Data in Enterprise Databases: Binding Corporate Data to the Wider World.* San Francisco: Morgan Kaufmann.

Churchman, C., and P. Ratoosh, eds. 1959. *Measurement: Definitions and Theories.* New York: Wiley.

Cochran, W. 1997. *Sampling Techniques.* 3d ed. New York: Wiley.

Codd, E. 1970. "A Relational Model of Data for Large Shared Data Banks." *Communications of the ACM* 13 (6): 377–387.

Codd, E. 1990. *The Relational Model for Database Management: Version 2.* Reading, Mass.: Addison-Wesley.

Corey, D. 1997. "Data Quality Improvement in the Military Health Services Systems and the U.S. Army Medical Department." In *Proceedings of the 1997 Conference on Information Quality*, 37–62. Cambridge, Mass.: MITIQ.

Corey, D., L. Cobler, K. Haynes, and R. Walker. 1996. "Data Quality Assurance Activities in the Military Health Services System." In *Proceedings of the 1996 Conference on Information Quality*, 127–153. Cambridge, Mass.: MITIQ.

CRG (Cambridge Research Group). 1997a. *Information Quality Assessment (IQA) Software Tool.* Cambridge, Mass.: Cambridge Research Group, Inc.

CRG (Cambridge Research Group). 1997b. *Integrity Analyzer: A Software Tool for Total Data Quality Management.* Cambridge, Mass.: Cambridge Research Group, Inc.

Cykana, P., A. Paul, and M. Stern. 1996. "DoD Guidelines on Data Quality Management." In *Proceedings of the 1996 Conference on Information Quality*, 154–171. Cambridge, Mass.: MITIQ.

Davidson, B., Y. Lee, and R. Wang, 2004. "Developing Data Production Maps: Meeting Patient Discharge Submission Requirement." *International Journal of Healthcare Technology and Management* 6 (2): 87–103.

Delone, W., and E. McLean. 1992. "Information Systems Success: The Quest for the Dependent Variable." *Information Systems Research* 3 (1): 60–95.

English, L. 1999. *Improving Data Warehouse and Business Information Quality: Methods for Reducing Costs and Increasing Profits.* New York: Wiley.

Eppler, M. 2003. *Managing Information Quality: Increasing the Value of Information in Knowledge-Intensive Products and Processes.* Berlin: Springer.

Eppler, M., and M. Helfert. 2004. "A Classification and Analysis of Data Quality Costs." In *International Conference on Information Quality.* Cambridge, Mass.: MITIQ.

Fetter, R. 1991. "Diagnosis Related Groups: Understanding Hospital Performance." *Interfaces* 21 (1): 6–26.

Firth, C. 1993. *Management of the Information Product.* Master's Thesis, Massachusetts Institute of Technology.

Fisher, C., and B. Kingma. 2001. "Criticality of Data Quality as Exemplified in Two Disasters." *Information and Management* 39 (2): 109–116.

Fisher, C., E. Lauria, I. Chengalur-Smith, and R. Wang. 2006. *Introduction to Information Quality.* Cambridge, Mass.: MITIQ.

Fox, C., A. Levitin, and T. Redman. 1995. "The Notion of Data and Its Quality Dimensions." *Information Processing and Management* 30 (1) (January): 9–19.

Gitlow, H., S. Gitlow, A. Oppenheim, and R. Oppenheim. 1989. *Tools and Methods for the Improvement of Quality.* Boston: Irwin.

Guy, D., D. Carmichael, and O. Whittington. 1998. *Auditing Sampling: An Introduction.* 4th. New York: Wiley.

Han, J., and M. Kamber. 2001. *Data Mining: Concepts and Techniques*. San Francisco: Morgan Kaufmann.

Hand, D., H. Mannila, and P. Smyth. 2001. *Principles of Data Mining*. Cambridge, Mass.: MIT Press.

Hauser, J., and D. Clausing. 1988. "The House of Quality." *Harvard Business Review* 66 (3): 63–73.

Helfert, M. 2002. *Proaktives Datenqualitätsmanagement in Data-Warehouse-Systemen—Qualitätsplanung und Qualitätslenkung*. Berlin: Logos Verlag.

Hernadez, M. A., and S. J. Stolfo. 1998. "Real-World Data Is Dirty: Data Cleansing and the Merge/Purge Problem." *Journal of Data Mining and Knowledge Discovery* 1 (2).

Huang, K., Y. Lee, and R. Wang. 1999. *Quality Information and Knowledge*. Upper Saddle River, N.J.: Prentice Hall.

Huh, Y. U., F. Keller, T. Redman, and A. Watkins. 1990. "Data Quality." *Information and Software Technology* 32 (8): 559–565.

Jackson, J. 1963. "Jobshop Like Queueing Systems." *Management Science* 10 (1): 131–142.

Jarke, M., M. Jeusfeld, C. Quix, and P. Vassiliadis. 1999. "Architecture and Quality in Data Warehouses: An Extended Repository Approach." *Information Systems* 24 (3): 229–253.

Johnson, J., R. Leitch, and J. Neter. 1981. "Characteristics of Errors in Accounts Receivable and Inventory Audits." *Accounting Review* 56 (2): 270–293.

Kahn, B., D. Strong, and R. Wang. 2002. "Information Quality Benchmarks: Product and Service Performance." *Communications of the ACM* 45 (4) (April): 184–192.

Kaplan, D., R. Krishnan, R. Padman, and J. Peters. 1998. "Assessing Data Quality in Accounting Information Systems." *Communications of the ACM* 41 (2) (February): 72–78.

Katz-Haas, R., and Y. Lee. 2002. "Understanding Hidden Interdependencies between Information and Organizational Processes in Practice." In *Proceedings of the Seventh International Conference on Information Quality* (ICIQ), 18–30. Cambridge, MA: MITIQ.

Katz-Haas, R., and Y. Lee. 2005. "Understanding Interdependencies between Information and Organizational Processes in Practice." In *Information Quality*, ed. R. Y. Wang et al. Armonk, N.Y.: M. E. Sharpe.

Krantz, D., R. Luce, P. Suppes, and A. Tversky. 1971. *Foundations of Measurement: Additive and Polynomial Representation*. London: Academic Press.

Kriebel, C. 1979. Evaluating the Quality of Information Systems. In *Design and Implementation of Computer Based Information Systems*, ed. N. Szysperski and E. Grochla, 29–43. Germantown, Pa.: Sijthtoff and Noordhoff.

Laudon, K. 1986. "Data Quality and Due Process in Large Interorganizational Record Systems." *Communications of the ACM* 29 (1) (January): 4–11.

Lee, Y. 2004. "Crafting Rules: Context-Reflective Data Quality Problem Solving." *Journal of Management Information Systems* 12 (3) (Winter): 93–120.

Lee, Y., L. Pipino, D. M. Strong, and R. Y. Wang. 2004. "Process-Embedded Data Integrity." *Journal of Database Management* 15 (1): 87–103.

Lee, Y., and D. M. Strong. 2004. "Knowing-Why about Data Processes and Data Quality." *Journal of Management Information Systems* 20 (3) (Winter): 13–49.

Lee, Y. W., D. M. Strong, B. K. Kahn, and R. Y. Wang. 2002. "AIMQ: A Methodology for Information Quality Assessment." *Information and Management* 40 (2): 133–146.

Levitin, A., and T. Redman. 1998a. "A Model of Data Life Cycles with Applications to Quality." *Information and Software Technology* 35: 217–224.

Levitin, A., and T. Redman. 1998b. "Data as a Resource: Properties, Implications, and Prescriptions." *Sloan Management Review* 40 (1) (Fall): 89–102.

Liepins, G., and V. Uppuluri, eds. 1990. *Data Quality Control: Theory and Pragmatics*. New York: Marcel Dekker.

Loshin, D. 2001. *Enterprise Knowledge Management: The Data Quality Approach*. San Francisco: Morgan Kaufmann.

Madnick, S. 1999. "Metadata Jones and the Tower of Babel: The Challenge of Large-Scale Semantic Heterogeneity." In *Proceedings of the 1999 IEEE Meta-Data Conference*. Los Alamitos, Calif.: IEEE.

Madnick, S., R. Wang, K. Chettayar, F. Dravis, J. Funk, R. Katz, C. Lee, Y. Lee, X. Xian, and S. Bhansali. 2005. "Exemplifying Business Opportunities for Improving Data Quality from Corporate Household Research." In *Information Quality*, ed. R. Y. Wang, E. M. Pierce, S. E. Madnick, and C. W. Fisher, 181–196. Armonk, N.Y.: M. E. Sharpe.

Madnick, S., R. Wang, and X. Xian. 2004. "The Design and Implementation of a Corporate Householding Knowledge Processor to Improve Data Quality." *Journal of Management Information Systems* 20 (3): 41–70.

Meehan, M. 2002. "Data's Tower of Babel." *Computerworld* (April 15): 40–41.

Miller, H. 1996. "The Multiple Dimensions of Information Quality." *Information Systems Management* 13 (2) (Spring): 79–82.

Missier, P., G. Lalk, V. Verykios, F. Grillo, T. Lorusso, and P. Angeletti. 2003. "Improving Data Quality in Practice: A Case Study in the Italian Public Administration." *Distributed and Parallel Databases International Journal* 3 (2) (March): 135–160.

Morey, R. 1982. "Estimating and Improving the Quality of Information in the MIS." *Communications of the ACM* 25 (5): 337–342.

Naumann, F. 2002. *Quality-Driven Query Answering for Integrated Information Systems*. New York: Springer.

Och, C., R. King, and R. Osborne. 2000. "Integrating Heterogeneous Data Sources Using the COIL Mediator Definition Language." In *Proceedings of the Symposium on Applied Computing, Como, Italy*, 991–1000. New York: ACM.

Olson, J. 2003. *Data Quality: The Accuracy Dimension*. San Francisco: Morgan Kaufmann.

Oman, R., and T. Ayers. 1988. "Improving Data Quality." *Journal of Systems Management* 39 (5) (May): 31–35.

Orr, K. 1998. "Data Quality and Systems Theory." *Communications of the ACM* 41 (2) (February): 66–71.

Paulson, L. 2000. "Data Quality: A Rising E-Business Concern." *IT Pro* 2 (4) (July–August): 10–14.

Pierce, E. 2004. "Assessing Data Quality with Control Matrices." *Communications of ACM* 47 (2) (February): 82–84.

Pierce, E. 2005. "What's in Your Information Product Inventory?" In *Information Quality*, ed. R. Y. Wang, E. M. Pierce, S. E. Madnick, and C. W. Fisher, 99–114. Armonk, N.Y.: M. E. Sharpe.

Pipino, L., and D. Kopcso. 2004. "Data Mining, Dirty Data, and Costs." In *International Conference on Information Quality*. Cambridge, Mass.: MITIQ.

Pipino, L., Y. Lee, and R. Wang. 2002. "Data Quality Assessment." *Communications of the ACM* 45 (4) (April): 211–218.

Price, H. 1994. "How Clean Is Your Data?" *Journal of Database Management* 5 (1): 36–39.

Redman, T. 1996. *Data Quality for the Information Age*. Boston: Artech.

Redman, T. 1998. "The Impact of Poor Data Quality on the Typical Enterprise." *Communications of the ACM* 41 (2) (February): 79–82.

Redman, T. 2001. *Data Quality: The Field Guide*. Boston: Digital Press.

Rob, P., and C. Coronel. 2000. *Database Systems: Design, Implementation and Management*. 4th ed. Cambridge, Mass.: Course Technology.

Scannapieco, M., B. Pernici, and E. Pierce. 2002. "IP-UML: Towards a Methodology for Quality Improvement Based on the IP-Map Framework." In *International Conference on Information Quality*, 279–291. Cambridge, Mass.: MITIQ.

Shankaranarayan, G., R. Y. Wang, and M. Ziad. 2000. "Modeling the Manufacture of an Information Product with IP-MAP." In *International Conference on Information Quality*, 1–16. Cambridge, Mass.: MITIQ.

Shankarnarayanan, G., M. Ziad, and R. Wang. 2003. "Managing Data Quality in Dynamic Decision Environments: An Information Product Approach." *Journal of Database Management* 14 (4) (October–December): 14–32.

Soler, S., and D. Yankelevich. 2001. "Quality Mining: A Data Mining Method for Data Quality Evaluation." *International Conference on Information Quality*, 162–172.

Storey, V., and R. Wang. 1998. "Modeling Quality Requirements in Conceptual Database Design." In *Proceedings of the 1998 Conference on Information Quality*, 64–87. Cambridge, Mass.: MITIQ.

Strong, D., Y. Lee, and R. Wang. 1997a. "Data Quality in Context." *Communications of the ACM* 40 (5) (May): 103–110.

Strong, D., Y. Lee, and R. Wang. 1997b. "Ten Potholes in the Road to Information Quality." *IEEE Computer* 30 (8) (August): 38–46.

Strong, D., and S. Miller. 1995. "Exceptions and Exception Handling in Computerized Information Processes." *ACM Transactions on Information Systems* 13 (2) (April): 206–233.

Tayi, G., and D. Ballou. 1999. "Examining Data Quality." *Communications of the ACM* 41 (2): 54–57.

Total Data Quality Management Research Program (TDQM). ⟨http://mitiq.mit.edu/⟩.

Tuomi, I. 2000. "Data Is More Than Knowledge." *Journal of Management Information Systems* 16 (3): 103–117.

Wand, Y., and R. Wang. 1996. "Anchoring Data Quality Dimensions in Ontological Foundations." *Communications of the ACM* 39 (11) (November): 86–95.

Wang, R. 1998. "A Product Perspective on Total Data Quality Management." *Communications of the ACM* 41 (2) (February): 58–65.

Wang, R., T. Allen, W. Harris, and S. Madnick. 2003. "An Information Product Approach for Total Information Awareness." *IEEE Aerospace Conference.*

Wang, R., H. Kon, and S. Madnick. 1993. "Data Quality Requirements Analysis and Modeling." In *The 9th International Conference on Data Engineering,* 670–677. Los Alamitos, Calif.: IEEE.

Wang, R., Y. Lee, L. Pipino, and D. Strong. 1998. "Manage Your Information as a Product." *Sloan Management Review* 39 (4): 95–105.

Wang, R., and S. Madnick. 1990. "A Polygen Model for Heterogeneous Database Systems: The Source Tagging Perspective." In *The 16th International Conference on Very Large Data Bases,* 519–538. San Francisco: Morgan Kaufmann.

Wang, R., M. Reddy, and H. Kon. 1995. "Toward Quality Data: An Attribute-Based Approach." *Decision Support Systems* 13: 349–372.

Wang, R., V. Storey, and C. Firth. 1995. "A Framework for Analysis of Data Quality Research." *IEEE Transactions on Knowledge and Data Engineering* 7 (4) (August): 623–640.

Wang, R., and D. Strong. 1996. "Beyond Accuracy: What Data Quality Means to Data Consumers." *Journal of Management Information Systems* 12 (4) (Spring): 5–34.

Wang, R., M. Ziad, and Y. Lee. 2001. *Data Quality.* Norwell, Mass.: Kluwer Academic.

Yamane, T. 1967. *Elementary Sampling Theory.* Englewood Cliffs, N.J.: Prentice Hall.

Index